I SAW SATAN FALL

This book is dedicated to the many kind people
who have supported the writing of it with their prayers.
Without their prayers
it would certainly never have been written.

I SAW SATAN FALL

The Ways of Spiritual Warfare

Benedict M. Heron OSB

Foreword by Bishop Ambrose Griffiths OSB

New Life Publishing
Luton

First published in 1997 by
New Life Publishing,
60 Wickstead Avenue
Luton, Beds. LU4 9DP

British Library Cataloguing in Publication Data

Heron, Benedict M.
I Saw Satan Fall

ISBN 0 9529159 1 X

Typesetting by New Life Publishing, Luton
Printed and Bound in Great Britain by
Biddles Limited, Guildford, Surrey.

Contents

Publisher's Acknowledgements

Scripture quotations are from the Revised Standard Version of the Bible, copyright 1946, 1952, 1971 by the Division of Christian Education of the National Council of the Churches of Christ in the USA. Used by permission.

Extracts taken from Healing in the Spirit by Fr J McManus published and copyright 1994 by Darton, Longman and Todd Ltd and used by permission of the publishers.

Extracts taken from Renewal and the Power of Darkness by Cardinal Suenens published and copyright 1983 by Darton, Longman and Todd Ltd and used by permission of the publishers.

Extracts taken from Angels - True Stories of How they Touch our Lives, by Hope Price, published by Macmillan General Books, 1993.

Passage reprinted from The Curé D'Ars by Abbe Francis Trochu, with kind permission of TAN Books, Rockford, Illinois, USA.

Extracts from the following publications are also used with kind permission:

Vatican Council II Documents, Austin Flannery OP, Dominican Publications.
Spiritual Warfare, Derek Prince, Derek Prince Ministries Int.
Irish Bishops' Statement 1993, Catholic Media Office.
Papal Statements, L'Osservatore Romano (English Edition).
Padre Pio - The True Story, Bernard Ruffin, Our Sunday Visitor Inc.USA.
Spiritual Exercises, St. Ignatius Loyola, Society of Jesus.
Catechism of the Catholic Church, Geoffrey Chapman,a Cassell Imprint
"Send me your Guardian Angel", Fr. Alessio Parente, OFM Cap

Foreword

Christ said of His disciples: "In my name they will cast out devils" and St. Paul warns us that we have to struggle "against the spiritual army of evil in the Heavens", but today there is little awareness of the power of Satan and very often any mention of the Devil and demons is treated with scepticism or complete disbelief.

We have been powerfully influenced by the secular society in which we live, but if we turn to the Scriptures we will be surprised by the frequent references to both good and bad Angels. This teaching is reinforced by the Constitutions on the Liturgy, and on the Church of the Second Vatican Council, by many texts in our Liturgy, and the very clear teaching of the Catechism of the Catholic Church.

The lives of many Saints contain accounts of attacks by the Devil and these are confirmed by the contemporary records of the life of Padré Pio. We should then surely be ready to accept the personal testimony of those who have witnessed cases of the powerful influence evil spirits can have over people and even cases of full possession by the Devil. Many of these cases arise through people dabbling in occult practices such as astrology, spiritualism, or magic, which illustrates the danger of such activities which can so easily fascinate people and get them deeply involved without their realising it.

FOREWORD

Occult practices are, in fact, very widespread today including witchcraft and actual satanism involving people giving their lives to Satan. The natural tendency is to deny the existence of such things for fear of being thought crazy, but this does not alter the facts nor prevent satanism from being present in much heavy metal music and so influencing many young people.

None of this should make us afraid because Jesus has power over all evil spirits and will always protect us if we have faith in Him. But we must play our part through prayer, through frequenting the Sacraments and making use of valuable pious practices which are too often neglected today. We can help others by praying for them to be delivered from evil spirits but any attempt at exorcism must be left to those specially appointed by the Bishop because it can easily be dangerous.

This book provides a wealth of information on all these topics and is a very timely reminder of the reality of the Devil and his demons at a time when he is close to his greatest triumph in making us think that he does not exist. It is equally important to avoid all exaggeration such as by those who condemn all alternative therapies as the work of the Devil. The truth is that there is no objection to the therapies themselves but it can happen that particular practitioners are under demonic influences and have a corresponding effect on those they treat.

The author throughout is very fair and balanced in his treatment, as in his discussion of the New Age Movement which is popular because of its concern for the environment, the protection of our planet, and for peace but contains many elements including reincarnation, astrology, and spiritualism wholly incompatible with orthodox Christian belief.

We are all engaged in a spiritual warfare and it is not fanciful to suspect demonic powers as contributory factors in much of the suffering and horrors perpetrated in recent years. It is vital that, while avoiding all exaggeration, we should be aware of the widespread and powerful influence of the Devil and should equally make full use of the means and power Jesus gives us to conquer him and to heal those who have fallen under his power.

Rt.Revd. Ambrose Griffiths, OSB
Bishop of Hexham and Newcastle

January 1997.

Acknowledgements

The writing of this book has been a very corporate activity. So many people have helped by sharing their experiences, by giving advice, by encouraging, and above all by praying, that although I personally actually wrote nearly all the book, yet I feel that in a sense it is 'our' book not 'my' book. So, very many thanks to all of those who helped.

Very warm thanks are due to my publishers, Gerard and Toni Pomfret of New Life Publishing, who could not have been more helpful in every way.

Special thanks are due to Joan Lewington, who cheerfully deciphered my impossible handwriting and typed the text, as well as rendering help in many other ways.

I gratefully thank Bishop Ambrose Griffiths OSB for his encouraging Foreword and helpful advice. Special thanks are also due to the anonymous French psychiatrist (Dr. F.) who wrote the invaluable chapter seven. Many thanks also to the priest exorcists who provided testimonies for chapter eight.

Over the years I consulted so many people about the contents of this book it would be impossible to remember all of them. However, I should like to express publicly my gratitude to the following for their kind help, with apologies to those whom I have mistakenly left out:

ACKNOWLEDGEMENTS

Father Luke Ballwegg OSB
Anne Barrett
Sister Regina Collins
Father Sean Conaty
Father Hubert Condron CP
Father Jack Finnegan
Father Jeremy Davies
Myles Dempsey
Erika Gibello
Father Michael Gwinnell
Father Peter Hocken
Father David Keniry
Father Michael Killeen
Francis MacNutt
Elizabeth McCavera
Sister Agnes McKeon
Fr James McManus CSSR
Bishop Maddocks
Dr. John Bonnici Mallia
Father Leonard May
Archbishop Milingo
The late Rev. Neil-Smith
Father Rufus Periera
Morag Reeve
The Rev John Richards
Vivien Sewell
Eileen Shaughnessy
Mary Tanner

and also Charles Whitehead, who not only advised helpfully, but who has kindly written the notice for the cover of the book.

Needless to say, I cannot claim that all the above people would approve of everything in the book, although in general I think they would very certainly do so.

Then I must thank my brother, Giles Heron and his wife Mary, whose knowledge of the English language is more refined than my own, and who helped to tidy up my style.

Many thanks are also due to my monastic community, who have allowed me the freedom to develop my healing ministry, and who have supported me in many other ways.

Benedict M. Heron OSB

January 1997

Introduction

There are three areas of evil which we are all called with God's grace to fight against: the world, the flesh, and the devil.

The world in this sense is the unjust and immoral pressures and structures which largely surround us: the rat race competition, the worship of money, the cult of sexual experience and pleasure, the couldn't-care-less attitude towards those in great need, such as the starving millions, and the rape of the environment.

The flesh is our fallen nature prone to sin, the tendency in each one of us to rebel against God and the laws of God. We need only think of the traditional seven capital or deadly sins of pride, covetousness, lust, anger, gluttony, envy, and sloth to realise directions in which we are tempted to go against the will of God.

Finally, there is the devil and his demons. The New Testament is definite in its teaching about the existence of the devil and his demons. Christian tradition is equally definite; and the official teaching of the Catholic Church today as seen in the documents of the Second Vatican Council, in the statements of the Popes, and in the new universal Catechism is no less definite. One should add that all the Eastern Orthodox churches and all the Evangelical and Pentecostal churches are quite sure that the devil and demons exist.

However, there are now Christians, including some Catholics, who deny that the devil and demons exist. There are other Christians who are uncertain, and there are still other Christians who simply forget this whole area of Christian doctrine and for whom, to all intents and purposes, the devil and demons do not exist, whatever they may claim to believe in theory.

There are doubtless areas of Christian doctrine which are fairly peripheral and which do not make much difference to our Christian understanding and life. However, the existence of the devil and demons is not peripheral. For if, as the Bible and the Catholic Church teach, we are all involved in spiritual warfare with demonic forces, then it is very important to know about it. If we are all at times being attacked by demonic forces, then it is vital to be aware of the fact, otherwise we cannot truly understand what is happening to us and counter it.

The devil and demons do not only attack individuals. They attack marriages, families, parishes, institutions, churches, nations, and the world. Again, I do not think that we can understand what is happening in families and groups, whether small or large, if we leave out of account the attacks of the devil. So, for example, I would think that the devil has clearly been active in the troubles in the royal marriages in our country recently - by attacking royal marriages, he strikes a strategic blow against the institution of marriage as a whole.

I would also think that we cannot fully understand the murdering of six million Jews by the Nazis if we leave out of account the demonic factor. If anyone had said in 1925 that within twenty five years six million Jews would be killed in Europe, he or she would have been told by everyone that such a thing was utterly and entirely impossible. But it happened. It is easier to understand the holocaust if we see it not just as the work of Hitler and some other evil men, but if we realise that the main instruments behind it were demonic forces working through sinful and weak men.

My conviction that we are all involved in spiritual warfare with demonic forces is not only based on the Bible and on the official teaching of the Catholic Church. It is also confirmed by personal experience - my own awareness of being attacked by the devil, but also my experience as a priest trying to help others, especially in the charismatic healing ministry. I have never been the official exorcist for a diocese, but in more than one diocese I have been called in to help priests who were officially involved in dealing with cases requiring the ministry of exorcism.

I have seen and heard things which pointed very much towards direct demonic activity, for instance, a loud aggressive masculine voice speaking obscenities, coming from the mouth of an apparently meek and pious woman. And I know two priests who in a particular case, with the bishop's permission, were together involved in exorcising a woman. As both priests told me, the woman levitated. And much more importantly, I have known people who were wonderfully and gloriously liberated and healed through the ministry of deliverance. I cannot help feeling that if some of the theologians who are demythologising the devil - that is to say, no longer believing in a personal devil - had seen and heard the things I have experienced and met some of the people I have met who were liberated by deliverance ministry, then they would perhaps think again.

In this book I am in the first place seeking to help people in the spiritual warfare in which we are all involved. This is not a specialist book on how to exorcise people, for I am not the right person to write such a book. It is primarily a book which seeks to help the ordinary Christian in his or her spiritual warfare. It is written especially with Catholics in mind, though I hope that other Christians will find it helpful. On the evangelical side there seems to be a spate of books appearing on the subject of spiritual warfare, but very little on the Catholic side. Spiritual warfare is basically the same whether viewed from a Catholic or an evangelical point of view. But there are differences of approach in certain areas and there is a need for Catholic literature on the subject.

Obviously many Protestants will not agree with everything written in this book, for example, the suggestion that it can be good to ask Our Lady to pray for us - which is not worshipping Mary! We do not have to agree, however, with everything in a book to benefit from reading it. I myself have considerably benefited from reading certain evangelical books with which I sometimes definitely disagreed in places. In true ecumenism we do not have to pretend that we agree about everything; we are not afraid openly to recognise and examine our differences. We do this, however, against the background of being fully and gratefully aware of our basic unity in Christ, which is far more important than our differences. So I hope that this book will contribute in its way to greater understanding and unity between Christians, especially between Catholics and Evangelicals.

Readers inevitably will find references to demons on many pages in this book, because of the nature of the subject. However, an important rule for spiritual warfare is that we should not be thinking and talking too much about the devil and demons. We should be aware that they exist; we should learn to recognise their activity and counter it; but our concentration should be very much on Jesus, who has overcome the evil one. The best way of dealing with the devil is to fall in love with Jesus; fill our minds with thoughts of him; let his holy name be frequently on our lips; give our lives entirely to him; and praise him with all our being, then we will have nothing to fear from the attacks of the devil. Let us with confidence remember the words of St. James: "Resist the devil, and he will flee from you" (James 4:7).

One last point: demons are fallen angels. Let us try to think about the good angels at least as much as we think about demons. Yes, we are attacked at times by demons, but we are also protected by good angels. Let us thank God for the protecting angels. Let us ask the angels to watch over us.

Chapter One

Angels and Demons in the New Testament

The Bible, especially the New Testament, is the basic source of Christian revelation. To know what to believe about angels and demons, we need above all to turn to the Bible, especially the New Testament. So in this chapter we are going to see in general what the New Testament says on this subject. I will quote from many passages and give numerous references, because I think this will have a cumulative effect. To understand the Christian revelation we need really to soak ourselves in God's word in Scripture. Going through these New Testament texts on angels and demons has been a real help to me as I prepared this chapter - it strengthened my faith, made my faith more real. I hope it will be the same for readers, even though references to such a large number of texts may seem rather daunting. It is important to remember here that we are not dealing with a few isolated references to angels and demons but with a multitude of texts.

An angel appeared to Joseph in a dream and said, "Joseph, son of David, do not be afraid to take Mary as your wife, for the child conceived in her is from the Holy Spirit. She will bear a son, and you are to name him Jesus, for he will save his people from their sins"

(Matthew 1:20). An angel also warned Joseph in a dream that Herod was seeking to kill Jesus, and that they should flee to Egypt (Matthew 1:13). Again in a dream, Joseph was told by an angel to return from Egypt, "for those who were seeking the child's life are dead" (Matthew 2:19).

The angel Gabriel appeared to Zechariah and spoke to him about the coming birth and mission of John the Baptist (Luke 1:11). It was also Gabriel who appeared to Mary and informed her about the coming birth of Jesus: "The Holy Spirit will come upon you, and the power of the Most High will overshadow you, therefore the child to be born will be holy; he will be called Son of God" (Luke 1:26). An angel of the Lord announces the birth of Jesus to the shepherds, and he is then joined by a multitude of the heavenly host, praising God and saying, "Glory to God in the highest heaven, and on earth peace among those whom he favours" (Luke 2:13).

"Angels came and waited on him" after Jesus' temptation in the desert, and an "angel from heaven appeared to him and gave him strength" (Luke 22:43) in Gethsemene. Angels are present at the resurrection of Jesus (Matthew 28:2; Luke 24:23; John 20:12).

In his teaching Jesus warns: "Take care that you do not despise one of these little ones; for, I tell you, in heaven their angels continually see the face of my Father in heaven" (Matthew 18:10). Jesus also said when arrested: "Do you think that I cannot appeal to my Father, and he will at once send me more than twelve legions of angels?" (Matthew 26:53). The angels are also ministers of God's judgement at the

Second Coming of Jesus (Matthew 13:41).

We again see the angels active in the Acts of the Apostles. Two angels speak to the disciples at the Ascension of Jesus (Acts 1:11). An angel rescues Peter and John from prison (Acts 5:19), and there is a lengthy account of an angel liberating Peter from prison in chapter 12 of Acts. An angel appears to Cornelius and tells him to send for Peter (Acts 10:3), and an angel tells Philip to take the road to Gaza, where he will meet the eunuch of the queen of Ethiopia (Acts 8:26). An angel appears to Paul in a dream during his voyage to Rome and assures him that all on the ship will be saved (Acts 27:23). "An angel of the Lord struck him down (Herod Agrippa) and he was eaten by worms and died" (Acts 12:32).

There are quite a number of references to angels in the New Testament epistles. For readers who wish to look them up, the references are: 1 Corinthians 4:9; 1 Corinthians 11:10; Galations 1:8; Galations 3:19; Colossians 2:18; 2 Thessalonians 1:7; 1 Timothy 5:21; Hebrews 1:4; Hebrews 2:2; 2 Peter 24; Jude 6. Finally, there are numerous references to angels in the last book of the Bible, Revelation. The following is a beautiful example: "And all the angels stood around the throne and around the elders and the four living creatures, and they fell on their faces before the throne and worshipped God singing, 'Amen! Blessing and glory and wisdom and thanksgiving and honour and power and might be to our God for ever and ever! Amen' (7:11)."

I have mentioned the above references in the New Testament to angels at some length because taken as a whole they surely give the idea of very real personal beings who speak and act. If one demythologises angels, then it is surely logical to also demythologise other things in the New Testament, such as the Virgin Birth of Jesus and his Resurrection, as also the dogma of the Incarnation, which of course is just what many very liberal Christians have done. Needless to say, Christians who demythologise angels - who do not believe in personal angels - also demythologise the devil and demons. So for such Christians there is no such thing as spiritual warfare against demonic beings - there are no such beings to fight against!

Now it is time to see what the New Testament says about the devil, also called Satan, and demons. "Jesus, full of the Holy Spirit, returned from the Jordan and was led by the Spirit in the wilderness, where for forty days he was tempted by the devil" (Luke 4:1). This is followed by the three special temptations, after which we read: "When the devil had finished every test, he departed from him until an opportune time."

When Peter attempts to dissuade Jesus from going to his Passion, Jesus rebukes him: "Get behind me, Satan!" (Matthew 16:23). Satan takes the seed of the word away from those who have received it (Mark 4:15). "The devil had already put it into the heart of Judas, son of Simon Iscariot, to betray him" (John 13:2), and after Judas "received the piece of bread, Satan entered into him" (John 13:25). Satan tries to sift the disciples like wheat (Luke 22:31).

The devil is the enemy who sows weeds in the field of the Lord's wheat (Matthew 13:39). "Satan bound for eighteen years" (Luke 13:16) a crippled woman. Jesus said: "I watched Satan fall from heaven like a flash of lightening. See, I have given you authority to tread on snakes and scorpions, and over all the power of the enemy; and nothing will hurt you" (Luke 10:18) - this followed the words of the seventy two, "Lord, in your name even the demons submit to us!"

There are of course quite a number of references in the New Testament to Jesus casting out demons. After he cured Peter's mother-in-law, we read: "That evening they brought to him many who were possessed with demons; and he cast out the spirits with a word, and cured all who were sick" (Matthew 9:16). There is the lengthy description of the casting out of the demons from the man in the country of the Gerasenes. The unclean spirits entered the pigs who rushed into the sea and were drowned (Mark 5:1). There was the casting out of the demon from the dumb man, when the pharisees said, "By the ruler of the demons he casts out the demons" (Matthew 9:32). Similarly, Jesus is accused of casting out demons by the power of Beelzebub when he frees and heals a demoniac who was blind and mute (Matthew 12:22).

The epileptic boy was healed instantly when "Jesus rebuked the demon, and it came out of him" (Matthew 17:14). The disciples asked, "Why could we not cast it out?" and were told that it was "Because of your little faith." There was the man with an unclean spirit in a synagogue who was delivered: "And the unclean spirit, convulsing him and crying with a loud voice, came out of him" (Mark 1:26). This last text will mean more to the many Christians in our times who have heard "crying with a loud voice" as demons left people.

There are also references to the devil and demons in the Acts of the Apostles and in the epistles. Peter said to Ananias: "Why has Satan filled your heart to lie to the Holy Spirit and to keep back part of the proceeds of the land?" (Acts 5:3). A girl at Philippi had a divining spirit, which was cast out by Paul (Acts 16:16). "The Sadducees say that there is no resurrection, or angel, or spirit; but the Pharisees acknowledge all three" (Acts 23:8). "Gentiles will turn from the power of Satan to God" (Acts 26:18). Satan tempts (1 Corinthians 7:5) and seeks to outwit us (2 Corinthians 2:11). He tries to ensnare us (2 Timothy 2:7 and 2 Timothy 2:26). "Satan disguises himself as an angel of light" (2 Corinthians 11:14).

"Some (widows) have already turned away to follow Satan" (1 Timothy 5:15). "Therefore to keep me (Paul) from being too elated, a thorn was given me in the flesh, a messenger of Satan to torment me, to keep me from being too elated" (2 Corinthians 12:7). Satan hindered Paul from making a journey to Thessalonica (1 Thessalonians 2:18). "The coming of the lawless one is apparent in the working of Satan, who uses all power, signs, lying wonders, and every kind of wicked deception for those who are perishing" (2 Thessalonians 2:8).

"Resist the devil, and he will flee from you" (James 4:7). "The God of peace will shortly crush Satan under your feet" (Romans 16:20). The children of God are distinguished from the children of the devil (1 John 3:10). "Everyone who commits sin is a child of the devil, for the devil has been sinning from the beginning. The Son of God was revealed for this purpose, to destroy the works of the devil" (1 John 2:8).

In the book of Revelation there are a number of references to the devil and demons. In Chapter 12 the dragon pursues the "woman clothed with the sun", who gives birth to a son. "And war broke out in heaven; Michael and his angels fought against the dragon. The dragon and his angels fought back, but they were defeated, and there was no longer any place for them in heaven. The great dragon was thrown down, that ancient serpent, who is called Devil and Satan, the deceiver of the whole world - he was thrown down to the earth and his angels were thrown down with him" (Revelation 12:7).

In Revelation chapter 20 an angel "seized the dragon, that ancient serpent, who is the Devil and Satan, and bound him for a thousand years, and threw him into the pit, and locked and sealed it over him, so that he would deceive the nations no more, until the thousand years were ended. After that he must be let out for a little while."

Later, "When the thousand years are ended, Satan will be released from his prison and will come out to deceive the nations at the four corners of the earth, Gog and Magog, in order to gather them for battle; they are as numerous as the sands of the sea. They marched up over the breadth of the earth and surrounded the camp of the saints and the beloved city. And fire came down from heaven and consumed them. And the devil who had deceived them was thrown into the lake of fire and sulphur, where the beast and the false prophet were, and they will be tormented day and night for ever and ever" (Revelation 20:7).

Other references to demons include Acts 19:13 (where the Jewish exorcists were routed by an evil spirit), 1 Corinthians 10:20, 1 Timothy 4:1, James 2:19. ("Even the demons believe - and shudder"), 1 Corinthians 15:24, Ephesians 1:21, Ephesians 3:10, Ephesians 6:12, 1 Peter 3:22. In Jude there is a reference to demons as fallen angels: "And the angels who did not keep their own position, but left their proper dwelling, he has kept in eternal chains in deepest darkness for the judgement of the great day" (verse 6).

Two New Testament texts are especially important for our theme of spiritual warfare and I will quote them in full. "Finally, be strong in the Lord and in the strength of his power. Put on the whole armour of God, so that you may be able to stand against the wiles of the devil. For our struggle is not against enemies of flesh and blood, but against the rulers, against the authorities, against the cosmic powers of this present darkness, against the spiritual forces of evil in the heavenly places. Therefore take up the whole armour of God, so that you may be able to withstand on that evil day, and having done everything, to stand firm. Stand therefore, and fasten the belt of truth around your waist, and put on the breastplate of righteousness. As shoes for your feet put on whatever will make you ready to proclaim the gospel of peace. With all of these, take the shield of faith, with which you will be able to quench all the flaming arrows of the evil one. Take the helmet of salvation, and the sword of the Spirit, which is the word of God" (Ephesians 6:10).

And, "Discipline yourselves, keep alert. Like a roaring lion your adversary the devil prowls around, looking for someone to devour. Resist him, steadfast in your faith, for you know that your brothers and sisters in all the world are undergoing the same kinds of suffering" (1 Peter 5:8).

If we do not accept the obvious sense of the New Testament texts on angels and demons as personal beings, what are we to make of the texts mentioned above? If the devil does not exist as a personal being, what sense can we make of a sentence such as "Like a roaring lion your adversary the devil prowls around, looking for someone to devour. Resist him, steadfast in your faith" (1 Peter 5:8). In Ephesians chapter 6 we are told to "stand against the wiles of the devil. For our struggle is not against flesh and blood, but against the rulers, against the authorities, against the cosmic powers of this present darkness, against the spiritual forces of evil in the heavenly places". What are the "wiles of the devil" if there is no devil? If "our struggle is not against enemies of flesh and blood", then what are we struggling against if not personal demonic forces? If personal angels do not exist, what sense can we make of the words of Jesus: "Take care that you do not despise one of these little ones; for, I tell you, in heaven their angels continually see the face of my Father in heaven" (Matthew 18:10)? If personal angels do not exist, then what happened in Gethsemene when "an angel from heaven appeared to him (Jesus) and gave him strength" (Luke 22:43)? Did Jesus suffer from an hallucination? Or if the angel is only a literary invention of the author, how do we know that other things in the New Testament are not literary inventions?

If the angel Gabriel did not appear to Mary and speak to her, because he does not exist, if his appearances in Luke's gospel are just a literary device, then why not also reject his messages as a literary invention? If it is right to dismiss his appearance, then surely one can also reject his message. And the same could apply to the messages to Joseph.

I think it is impossible or at least illogical to demythologise the New Testament in this way without affecting basic truths of the Christian revelation. If we demythologise angels and demons it is logical also to demythologise the Virgin Birth, the Resurrection of Jesus, and the dogma of the Incarnation. Jesus becomes a good man and spiritual teacher, on the same level as Buddha. The Bible is more or less to be read like the Buddhist scriptures. A Dutch seminarian once said to me that he thought Jesus was the way for the West and Buddha for the East. So Christianity becomes one religion among many, more or less on the same footing as the others. That is, alas, exactly what has happened to the faith of many Christians.

I have no difficulty in understanding this 'comparative religion' position - it was my own view of things until I was twenty two. I attended school chapel in an Anglican boarding school twice a day for six years - under protest! - and I refused to be confirmed as an Anglican, because I did not believe in the divinity of Christ and all the other 'unscientific myths'. When reading St. John's Gospel at the age of twenty two I had by the grace of God a conversion experience, a conversion which was spiritual, moral, and intellectual. I found that I believed in the divinity of Christ: I believed that "In the beginning was the Word, and the Word was with God, and the Word was God" (John 1:1). I believed that, "before Abraham was, I Am" (John 8:58). I believed that, "I Am the vine and you are the branches", and the rest of John chapter 15.

I am not of course saying that the belief in the existence of personal angels and demons is the central truth of the Christian revelation. I am saying, however, that once you start demythologising angels and demons you logically tend to go further, until you are at least doubting truths like the Virgin Birth, the Resurrection, and the Incarnation.

I think we Catholics can learn from what is happening in the Protestant world. The Evangelicals, whatever their mistakes or limitations may sometimes be, tend to have a much firmer and more vital faith than the liberal Protestants, whose Christian belief often becomes uncertain and nebulous.

One final point: the Christian religion is not only for learned intellectuals, indeed Jesus seemed to have a special love and concern for the simple and the poor. To read the New Testament through demythologising spectacles would demand an intellectual training well beyond that of the great majority of the people in the world today. So the New Testament would become a book which was really only open to the learned, which is clearly not right for the sacred book of the religion founded by Jesus, who preached good news to the poor. There are not two Christian revelations, two Christian creeds, one for the learned, one for the rest. One does not have to be a fundamentalist to accept the teaching of the New Testament and the Church at their face value. After looking at the New Testament, some readers may now like to jump to Appendix 1, to see what the official teaching and documents of the Catholic Church say about angels and demons. It would of course be equally possible to quote also from the official documents of other churches, for example, the Eastern Orthodox and Pentecostals, but that would be going beyond the scope of this small book.

Chapter Two

Demonic Attacks

We have seen what the New Testament has to say about angels and demons. Let us now try to understand what all this means in practice in the lives of each one of us. How does being involved in spiritual warfare manifest itself in my life, in your life, in the lives of people around us, in the lives of the inhabitants of England at the end of the twentieth century, and at the global world level?

Individuals

As an individual, I am the object of God's infinite love, of Jesus' saving grace, of the prayers of Our Lady and the saints, of the protecting presence of the angels, and of the attacks of demonic forces, of the "flaming darts of the evil one" (Ephesians 6:16). These demonic attacks vary greatly in intensity and frequency. As John Richards has said, they can be compared to a long thin wedge. At the thick end of the wedge there are things like demonic possession, Satanism, and specially powerful attacks of the devil. At the thin end of the wedge there are the small daily temptations in which our own sinfulness is often worked on by demonic darts. And there is the whole range of gradually increasing demonic attacks in between the two extremes.

Perhaps an analogy can help us here. We can say that someone is troubled by sickness. This can vary in seriousness from the beginnings of a cold to terminal cancer. So if we say that someone is sick we want to know where it is on the long thin wedge of sickness, so to speak. Similarly, if we say that someone is being attacked by the devil - we all are - we need to know how serious is the attack, how far down the wedge it is. Theologians sometimes distinguish between the ordinary attacks of the devil and the extraordinary attacks. Certainly one can say that many temptations are just ordinary attacks, and that cases of possession are extraordinary ones. But there is an in-between area where it can be difficult to distinguish between the ordinary and the extraordinary.

Sometimes a person will say to me that he thinks he or someone else is being attacked by the devil. I frequently reply that he certainly is, because we all are. Then I ask him to tell me more about it, so that we can seek to understand how seriously and in what way the devil may be attacking him. Perhaps the particular thing which is troubling him is mainly a matter of imagination or a psychological problem, but the devil can also be involved in these.

Is every temptation the result of direct demonic attack? I am not prepared to say so. Doubtless many temptations are just due to our weakness and sinfulness. How do we know whether or not there is an element of direct demonic attack in a temptation? I tend to say that when a temptation is unduly strong and tenacious, unduly difficult to get rid of, then we can think that the weakness and sinfulness of our nature is not the only thing involved, but that the flaming darts of the evil one are there, playing on our weakness and sinfulness.

Thus, if someone is experiencing strong temptations or trials of, for example, anger, pride, lust, fear, discouragement, or alcoholism, especially when there is no apparent cause for the strength of the temptation or trial, then I would think that some degree of direct demonic attack is involved. I would add that I do not think the devil normally wastes flaming darts on areas of our lives where we have no problems and are strong. Thus if someone has no inclination towards sexual promiscuity or alcoholism, and is strong in these areas, then doubtless the devil will normally find it more profitable to send his flaming darts on other areas where that person is weaker and where there is an opening.

Furthermore, the devil does not only trouble people with flaming darts. He can have a grip on one or more areas of our lives, where we are in a state of lesser or greater demonic bondage. Where someone has a serious drink or drug problem, when someone has a really uncontrollable temper, or is seriously involved in adulterous activity or pornography, when someone is worshipping money or is always hyper-critical, when someone is strongly tempted to suicide, or suffers from serious spiritual pride, when someone is really involved in the occult, then there is normally an element of demonic bondage present. That does not mean that the person is not in a state of grace or is possessed by the devil - someone can be crippled in one area of their life but be alright in others. We have all met people with, say, a drink or a sexual problem who were truly generous and kind to others. It is good to remember that "love covers a multitude of sins" (1 Peter 4:8).

The demonic bondage mentioned above is often called demonic oppression or obsession or infestation. The devil has partial control of the person, leaving other areas of their lives free from his control. This is something different from full demonic possession, where the devil has complete control of the human personality which is, thank God, much rarer than demonic oppression. One very experienced and gifted exorcist says that in his experience full possession only seems to take place when a person hands over his or her will completely to the power and authority of the devil. However, the boundary between a very serious oppression and possession may not in practice be always easy to distinguish - one can more or less drift into the other. The seriousness of demonic oppression can vary greatly.

The Family and Smaller Groups

The devil attacks not only individuals, but also families and other smaller groups. When in a family or small group everything starts going wrong and misunderstandings arise; when people start getting on each other nerves; when normally calm people begin to explode with anger; when people become deeply suspicious of each other: then we can surely think that the family or group is under special demonic attack.

In my opinion the devil normally plays an important part in the break up of marriages. The seemingly endless misunderstandings, suspicions, tensions, bickerings, and strife in some marriages between people who are not basically evil and who are trying, up to a point, to be loyal and loving, is surely not something which can be fully understood if we leave out of account the flaming darts of the devil. Then of course there are the marriages where there is serious evil on one side or the other, or both, and there the work of the devil is more obvious.

All these troubles in marriages and families can be complicated by things like emotional, mental, or physical illness, and by the loss of jobs, and by accidents of one kind or another. People can experience a run of 'bad luck'. Demons can play their part in all this, indeed they normally do. The devil seeks to prevent people from doing the work for the Kingdom which God wants them to do. One can have the impression that an evil unseen force is orchestrating the attack on an individual marriage, a family, a group, and that the consideration of the human factors mentioned above is not sufficient to understand what is happening.

The same applies to other groups like schools, businesses, and health service units. It also applies to Christian groups such as parishes, prayer groups, and religious communities. Anyone who has lived for long in a monastery will know that sometimes the community seems to run into a difficult period without there being any obvious explanation for it. Similarly, a prayer group which has been going along happily will suddenly find tensions and personality clashes rearing their heads. These things cannot, in my opinion, be fully understood if one leaves out of account the attacks of the devil.

The Nation and the World

The ills of our country and of the world are obvious to anyone who reads a newspaper or looks at the news on television. Wars, violence, crime, injustice, oppression and exploitation of the weak, abortions, sexual immorality, child abuse, racism, the breakdown of marriages, alcoholism and drug abuse, irreligion, needless cruelty to animals, abuse of the environment, lack of freedom - the list could be continued - are obvious signs of real trouble in society. If the devil exists, which he does, if he has some power, which he has within the limits that God permits, obviously he will play his part in the many problems and crises of our country and our world. Just imagine for a moment that you were Satan! Obviously you would do everything you could to cause destruction, hate, dis-unity, violence, despair, immorality, false religion, and the spreading of lies at every level. And Satan does just that!

He is normally at work when decisions are taken which lead to wars, when politicians or generals needlessly escalate the violence, when criminals murder the innocent, when people commit suicide, when the hungry are left to starve, when a blind eye is turned towards the homeless, when young girls are lured into prostitution, when drug pushers ensnare the young, when a father sexually abuses his child, when greedy people rape the environment for money, when there is atheist propaganda in schools, when people torture animals for fun, when women are socially oppressed, when the rich grow richer and the poor grow poorer within a country or between countries, and when people really blaspheme against God. Again, the list could be extended.

Some people will object that in this chapter I am bringing the devil into situations and ills which can be sufficiently explained by natural causes. Thus, it will be said, a woman committed suicide because she was depressed after the death of her husband; that someone sexually abused his child because he himself was sexually abused by his father; that two countries went to war because of a clash of economic interests; that men oppress women because in their culture they were brought up to do so. Certainly natural explanations can have a validity at their own level. It is not, however, a matter of asking whether this or that ill was caused by natural and human causes or by the devil. Obviously, the devil works largely through natural causes. But whether certain natural and human causes lead to a disaster or whether the disaster is avoided can depend on the spiritual battle going on in the background. The reason why one depressed spouse commits suicide and another does not can be because one knows how, with God's grace, to resist the attacks of the devil and the other does not.

The Christian Community

Finally, one area where particularly sadly the devil is at work is within the Christian community. An obvious example of this is Christian dis-unity and hostility among Christians. Another area is worldliness among

Christians. Yet another is false doctrine - we can all agree that this is so, even though we do not agree as to what is false doctrine! Perhaps the devil is particularly concerned to attack the Christian community, because by doing so he places obstacles in the way of the Christian message to the world, for the world itself can only be saved by the gospel of Jesus.

It is not difficult now to recognise that the devil was at work when Catholics were killing Protestants for being Protestants, and vice versa; when Christians were violently persecuting Jews; when Christians were defending the institution of slavery. What we in the Christian community have to do now is to ask ourselves, humbly and prayerfully, where today the devil is having his way with us; where today he is especially attacking us. We may not concentrate all our efforts on combating the work of the devil in the world and neglect his actions among the Christian community. Indeed, we need to pay special attention to his influence on the followers of Jesus.

Part of the difficulty of resisting demonic attacks is that most of them are not recognised as such even by many Christians. Someone feels a compulsion to go out and get drunk or to gamble; someone bursts into an angry rage and shouts at their children or hits them; someone steals at the supermarket; someone buys a pornographic magazine: all of this usually without the thought of the devil ever crossing their mind. And the same applies to politicians who make unjust decisions and pursue unjust policies. Doubtless the devil prefers it that way. Doubtless he is normally happier not be recognised but to work in a hidden and secret way - there is less danger of stirring up opposition if he is unrecognised.

However, there are times when the devil's presence and activity is recognised as such. This may be partly a question of sensitivity but it seems to happen especially to two groups of people. The first group is composed of people who are trying very seriously to serve God. They will be very especially attacked by the devil, since they are particularly dangerous for his kingdom. In Appendix Two we will see examples of holy people being dramatically attacked by the devil and Chapter Five of this book seeks to help Christians to combat the attacks of the devil.

The second group is mainly composed of people who have got seriously involved in the occult. They can then begin to experience in one way or another the presence of demonic forces. This may well be very frightening for them, and some of them will come to a priest seeking deliverance. I think of a Catholic woman who came to me seeking help after getting deeply involved in the attempt to develop psychic powers through non-Christian meditation. This had led to a period in a psychiatric hospital, where they could not understand the cause of her trouble. Very strange things were happening in her flat, including the feeling of extreme coldness. She ended up by seeing the diocesan exorcist. It is now time to consider the whole question of the occult at greater length.

Chapter Three

The Occult, Witchcraft, and Satanism

"When you come into the land that the Lord your God is giving you, you must not learn to imitate the abhorrent practices of those nations. No one shall be found among you who makes a son or daughter pass through fire, or who practices divination, or is a soothsayer, or an augur, or a sorcerer, or one who casts spells, or who consults ghosts or spirits, or who seeks oracles from the dead. For whoever does these things is abhorrent to the Lord." (Deuteronomy 18:9).

Human beings are not just animals. There is a spiritual side to our being. When people turn away from true religion, they tend to get involved in false spiritual ways - and this is happening on a large scale in our country and in some others also, as people have moved away from their Christian roots.

There is an exciting side to a vital Christianity as people have a living relationship with Jesus; as they experience answers to prayer; as they become aware that the Holy Spirit is guiding them. All this does not, as some may think, do away with the Cross, rather it helps us to bear the Cross fruitfully. For example, St. Paul was wonderfully blessed with visions and special divine illuminations, and gifts of healing, which were of vital importance to the fruitfulness of his ministry, yet of course he suffered much.

I think that in our times God seems to be being

especially generous with spiritual gifts, experiences, and illuminations, perhaps particularly but not only in the context of the Charismatic Renewal. However, many people today are not open to receiving their spiritual support and uplift from Christian sources, so they seek them elsewhere, and increasingly often from occult sources.

So people get involved with astrology, often to the point of consulting the stars before making all significant decisions. Or they will go to a spiritualist medium, or palmist, or a clairvoyant to seek guidance. Or they will seek healing from witches. Or they will ask a magician to curse someone for them. Or they will dedicate their life to Satan to obtain such things as perverted sexual pleasure, money, and power over others.

Of course, reading your horoscope in the newspaper or reading tea leaves is vastly different from being involved in satanism - just as pinching an apple from a shop is very different from being involved in raiding banks. However, all involvement in the occult is wrong, just as all stealing is wrong. Small scale stealing can eventually lead to serious crime, and a slight flirting with the occult can drift into serious involvement.

The occult can exercise a growing fascination on people, especially people who have no serious religious commitment. It opens people up to a mysterious new world, which can appear to promise exciting rewards. I remember reading an occult advertisement in a magazine which promised to teach people to make members of the opposite sex fall in love with them, to make their business prosper, to bring healing, and to enable them to get rid of an unwanted neighbour.

I think one can get deeply involved in the occult without being an evil person. I knew a woman who became a spiritualist medium and often engaged in astral travel. She owned and directed a small nursery school, but as a result of her occult involvement she soon could not cope with running the school and she was cracking up. She was never in my opinion an evil person, but she had got really entangled with evil spirits. Two of us prayed with her for healing over a period of a few months and evil spirits came out of her. She became a serious Christian, gave up all involvement with the occult, and was able happily to run her school again.

I remember another woman who had joined a white witches group. She said that she had joined them to help fight black witchcraft and to help heal people. After some years she realised that she had got caught up with demonic forces. After a few months' healing ministry, which also involved casting out evil spirits, she was freed. When she first came to us she was a lapsed Catholic, and now she is a very fervent one, doing work of national importance as a social worker. When she first came she had a glazed look in her eyes; now her eyes sparkle with the light which comes from Jesus. She again, in my opinion, was never an evil person - she would never have wanted to harm anyone. But as she herself realised, she certainly had got seriously entangled with evil spirits.

I do not wish to suggest that everyone who has had

their palm read at a fair, or visited a clairvoyant, has as a result picked up an evil spirit. But I do think that all serious involvement with the occult results in some degree of demonic bondage, and even a one-off occult experience can sometimes result in serious demonic problems. A teenage boy from Yorkshire savagely killed a nine year old girl after seeing the film, The Exorcist. He said: "It was not really me that did it, you know: there was something inside me. I want to see a priest. It is ever since I saw that film, The Exorcist. I felt something take possession of me. It has been in me ever since."

As a teenager, before I became a Catholic, I like many other people and out of curiosity flirted with the occult. Two people cast my horoscope, a clairvoyant crystal gazer had a picture of me which later came to pass, a few people read my palm, and I disgraced myself by getting a fit of the giggles in a spiritualist church service. When I became a Catholic and made my first general confession, I did not confess these occult activities - no one ever suggested that there might be such a need. Years later as a priest involved in Charismatic Renewal I confessed this occult involvement and received cleansing prayer. However, I do not think that my occult involvement had actually resulted in demonic trouble - perhaps my guardian angel was protecting me. But it was right to confess it and receive cleansing prayer. There may be some readers of this book who would also be wise to confess past activities of this kind and receive cleansing prayer, even if their involvement in the occult had only been slight. They should not be anxious about a slight past involvement in the occult, but it would be better to get it dealt with. (A cleansing prayer may be one which simply asks Jesus to cleanse us from any evil influence coming from past involvement with the occult. However, serious involvement with the occult may require a stronger prayer confronting evil spirits.)

The new Catechism of the Catholic Church has an excellent passage on the subject of the occult, which, it is to be hoped, will put an end to doubts which some Catholics may have had on this subject:

Divination and Magic

2115 "God can reveal the future to his prophets or to other saints. Still, a sound Christian attitude consists in putting oneself confidently into the hands of Providence for whatever concerns the future, and giving up all unhealthy curiosity about it. Improvidence, however, can constitute a lack of responsibility.

2116 "All forms of divination are to be rejected: recourse to Satan or demons, conjuring up the dead, or other practices falsely supposed to 'unveil' the future. Consulting horoscopes, astrology, palm reading, interpretation of omens and lots, the phenomena of clairvoyance, and recourse to mediums, all conceal a desire for power over time, history and, in the last analysis, other human beings, as well as a wish to conciliate hidden powers. They contradict the honour, respect, and loving fear that we owe to God alone.

2117 "All practices of magic or sorcery, by which one attempts to tame occult powers, so as to place them at one's service and have a supernatural power over others - even if this were for the sake of restoring their health - are gravely contrary to the virtue of religion. These practices are even more to be condemned when accompanied by the intention of harming someone, or when they have recourse to the intervention of demons. Wearing charms is also reprehensible. Spiritism often implies divination or magical practices; the Church for her part warns the faithful against it. Recourse to so-called traditional cures does not justify either the invocation of evil powers, or the exploitation of another's credulity."

Witchcraft

Witchcraft became legal in our country in 1951 and since then it has gown rapidly, so that it is calculated that there are now more than 250,000 witches in Britain. Witches very often regard witchcraft as a religion, the name which they usually give it being Paganism.

I was once asked at short notice to participate in a three hour television programme on witchcraft. I declined, rightly I think, but I stayed up late into the night to watch it. One young white witch was trying to present witchcraft as a respectable alternative religion, and she complained bitterly of discrimination against witches, as when one of her friends lost her job because her employer discovered she was a witch. The T.V. witch insisted that witches harmed no one.

However, her concentration must have slipped as the night went on, for she suggested later that a leading male English witch who had just died, may have died as a result of being cursed by the Scottish witches, who were angry with him for having revealed secrets of witchcraft in a book he had written. So these innocent witches may have killed a fellow witch by cursing him!

All witches believe in the power of charms and spells - indeed witchcraft is largely about exercising this power. What are we to think of this claim to spiritual power through charms, spells, and curses? From my experience and from consulting people from this and other countries, I have not the slightest doubt that spells and curses do have power, can really affect people, including people who do not know that they have been the object of spells and curses. I am even more certain however that Jesus can protect his followers from any and every spell and curse, even though they may sometimes have to pass through a difficult time.

Last year I spoke with an English Catholic doctor who had been working in the Pacific islands. Quite a number of times people who had been cursed would be brought to the hospital. There was nothing wrong with them physically, but they simply and rapidly faded away and died. He said to me how frustrating it was. He would tell them with vigour that there was no medical reason for them to die - but they did die! A missionary from Nigeria told me of a similar case, in which a healthy young man at the university after being cursed by a witch simply declined and died within two weeks. A member of our monastic community who comes from Ghana assures me that witch doctors' curses and spells in that country can have real power to harm, including harming people who do not know that they have been cursed. (A Dutch medical anthropologist working in Ghana confirmed this.) A Catholic doctor in this country consulted me about the case of a woman here who had been cursed by another woman at work - and the health of the first woman collapsed and remained collapsed in a way which was medically inexplicable.

A Catholic man from the third world came to us one evening seeking help. He had been a university lecturer and indeed a government minister in his country. His wife, from whom he has separated, was very deeply involved in witchcraft and she had got him cursed by 'experts'. His life was now in a state of total disarray and he could not concentrate to read a book or write letters - and there were other very difficult problems. In the name of Jesus we prayed against all curses and demonic attacks. He was immediately much better, and after a few more sessions he was able to work normally again. He then got a responsible job in an organisation helping the third world.

In nearly all third world countries the people living there seem to believe in the power of curses and spells. Indeed, their lives may become an existence of fear and misery, unless they have a truly living faith in Jesus. Increasingly also in our own country and the rest of the first world, people are coming up against the power of the occult and witchcraft. How sad it is to find Catholics, including some priests, who do not believe in the existence of demons and who therefore are not able fully to help so many needy people.

Doubtless quite a proportion of the people who come for this sort of help are just imagining things. But there are certainly many others who are not just imagining. On a number of occasions I have thought it was all imagination and psychological sickness, only to find out later that I was wrong. (A lonely widow from the third world came to us for help on account of the voices she was hearing. We prayed. the voices continued and I thought she was simply suffering from schizophrenia. However a very gifted and experienced Anglican exorcist prayed with her, delivered her from one or more evil spirits, and the voices ceased.)

White witchcraft is certainly much less evil than black witchcraft, but all witchcraft is evil and can open people up to the demonic. I remember reading about the altar of a famous white witch. The contents on the altar included a whip. There is often dancing around in the nude at witches ceremonies and self-flagellation or flagellation by others can play a part in this, especially it seems at initiation ceremonies.

On the television programme mentioned earlier the white witch was repeatedly asked if there had been sex at her initiation ceremony, but she simply refused to reply. However an ex-witch, now a serious Catholic, on the same programme said that she had been raped at her initiation ceremony. There were also questions about the ritual sexual abuse of children at witches' gatherings, the white witch replying that if such things happened it was only in very fringe groups who were not really witches.

White witches may talk about harming no one, but it is clearly all too easy for the white to become grey, and increasingly darker shades of grey, until it becomes black. When white witchcraft is no longer giving much of a kick, then people can easily seek something darker and stronger.

Satanism

Satanists tend to despise white witches, rather as a whisky drinker might despise those who stick to larger; or a heroine addict might look down on someone who went no further than cannabis. So let us look at the 'real thing'.

There are Christians who seem to doubt the existence of satanists, which is very strange, since some satanist groups make no secret of their existence, though they are very secretive about much of their activity. Anton LaVey, who founded The Church of Satan in the U.S.A. in 1966 and who is the author of the Satanic Bible, is a public figure in the USA. The Church of Satan is officially registered there as a religion, and they have branches in other countries, including this country - we also have our own satanist groups in Britain. LaVey has written: "Satan represents all of the so-called sins as they all lead to physical, mental, or emotional gratification!" Satanist Black Masses, performed on the body of a nude woman, can start with a prayer calling upon Satan, for example: "In nomine Dei nostri Satanas Luciferi excelsi." (In the name of our God Satan Lucifer glorious). Satanists are very fully and very explicitly anti-Christian, so the

Black Mass is deliberately a parody of the Catholic Mass. Sex and blood seem to play important parts in their rituals.

Satanists are accused of sexual orgies and rape, of ritual and sexual abuse of children, of torturing their victims, and of human sacrifices, including the procuring and eating of foetuses.

A senior C.I.D. police officer informed me that these things certainly do happen, but doubtless not as widely as some people claim. It cannot be affirmed that every satanist group is involved in the above activities. Obviously it is very difficult to obtain the sort of proof that would be required in a law court. A therapist can be quite right in judging that a particular child has been the object of ritual sexual abuse, while the police rightly decide that there is not enough evidence to procure a condemnation in a law court.

A priest told me of a case with which he was involved. A woman came to him for help in leaving a satanic coven to which she belonged - those who leave can be threatened with death. He did his best to help her. Some time later he received a letter from the satanist coven written in the woman's blood, threatening to kill him if he continued to help her. The coven had blackmailed her into returning by threatening to harm her son. The priest had not felt able to inform the police because the woman herself when a satanist had been involved in criminal acts. It can often be very difficult legally to do anything about such cases. Apparently in this one the woman was eventually allowed to leave the coven after being tortured. (Since writing the above paragraph, I have heard of a priest exorcist in the U.S.A. who has received death threats, so he now keeps his telephone number a secret.)

Satanism, like white witchcraft, is certainly spreading in our country and elsewhere, and it touches all levels of society. Some satanist groups try, it is said, to recruit especially among more educated and influential people. A report in the Guardian of February 8th 1994 mentions a court case in which a male witch had killed a satanist, Chris Rogers, with whom he was sharing a bed. The witch said that Rogers was really evil and had killed other people. The satanist, Chris Rogers, was at the time of his death deputy chairman of Manchester City Council's education committee. No comment needed! Satanists have certainly infiltrated into influential positions.

An area where there unquestionably has been much Satanist infiltration is the world of heavy metal rock groups. LaVey deliberately sought to enter the pop world, as a way of spreading satanism more quickly than could be achieved by the multiplication of satanist covens alone. Subliminal satanic messages have been included in rock records. Satanic messages can also be heard sometimes if the music is played backwards. At large pop gatherings the devotees are sometimes encouraged to close their fists, but straighten the index and little finger. The fist is then continually raised up and down in the air as a salute to Satan, the two straightened fingers representing Satan's horns. The satanist orientation of some of the songs is entirely open. So also are the occult and satanist symbol on the sleeves of records and elsewhere, for example the inverted cross, the five point star (the pentagram), the number of the beast '666', the goat's head and horns. Christians will find especially offensive the blasphemous songs and scenes, such as mock crucifixions.

When one remembers the large numbers of young people involved in the heavy metal rock scene, then surely we Christians should be deeply concerned. I spoke with one young woman who had before her conversion been involved for a number of years with this sort of music. She told me that evil spirits had certainly got a hold on her at that time. How many other young people are suffering from some form of demonic oppression as a result of heavy metal rock? And how well prepared is the Catholic Church for helping them?

A very challenging book has recently been published in England, 'Treating Survivors of Satanist Abuse', edited by Valerie Sinason (Routledge), in which a considerable number of psychiatrists and psychotherapists discuss their experiences and give advice. The authors have, usually very reluctantly, come to the conclusion that satanic ritual abuse of children and others is unquestionably taking place - they give case histories. They also point out that most people seem to be frightened of facing up to this fact.

The Guardian (6th September 1992) published an article reporting that in Soweto small boys were being kidnapped, having their testicles and thumbs cut off, and being left to die, so that witchdoctors could use these parts of their bodies to make magic potions. The thought that such a thing takes place in South Africa is bad enough, but to face the fact that things not much less terrible could be happening in England is too much for many people.

I think that fear prevents large numbers of people from seeing things objectively in the whole realm of the satanic - fear operating in so many ways. Fear of facing up to the existence of pure evil; fear of being regarded as superstitious or crazy by other people; fear of being the object of demonic curses; fear of getting involved with something one cannot cope with. A social worker, a school teacher, a doctor, a policeman, or a lawyer, could all fear that, for example, recognising the existence of satanic abuse in a particular case could involve them in an immense amount of work, criticism, and jeopardise their careers. It might also cause them to fear for their personal safety and that of their families. They may well think that if satanic curses perhaps do have some power, then it would be better not to be on the receiving end of them.

A priest can also have to face the problem of his own fears when confronting some demonic problems, as I know very well from my own personal experience. One priest exorcist whom I know was protected only by spiritual power when someone held a knife to his throat. Another priest exorcist turned round just in time when a woman was approaching him from behind with scissors. An Anglican priest exorcist friend of mine was knocked over by a woman he was seeking to liberate from evil spirits.

Fear, however, normally operates in much more subtle ways. Fear of being ridiculed and regarded as a relic from the Middle Ages; fear of being blamed if something goes wrong; fear of anything getting into the press; fear of getting involved with cases which will take up much time and energy; fear of one's health being affected. I personally have experienced several of the above fears.

So there are very often strong human pressures in favour of deciding it cannot be satanic - it must be the imagination or inventions of unbalanced people. And in any case it would be very imprudent to get personally involved in this matter, especially since one is already very busy with other things. The result of all this is that desperately needy people may not be helped and that more people may continue to become victims of incredible cruelty.

Is there no danger of some people going over the top and seeing devils where there are none; of thinking that people have suffered from satanic ritual abuse when they have not? Yes, such dangers certainly exist. And one may not forget that in past centuries some innocent people in our country were burned to death for being witches when they were not.

However, I think that in our times much the bigger danger is the non-recognition of the satanic. Some evangelical Christians have doubtless exaggerated. But I think that on the whole we need to be grateful to the evangelicals for reminding us that the devil exists, that he is still active in our times, and that Jesus gave to his church a ministry of casting out devils. Perhaps some of us who have just wanted to play safe need to repent. I personally have to repent of sometimes having taken a safety first or safety at any price approach in the past.

Chapter Four

The New Age Movement and Alternative Therapies

The New Age Movement is not an organisation with a registered membership. It is a loose collection of individuals and groups who tend to share certain basic beliefs and practices. There are recognised centres, like the Findhorn Foundation in Scotland, and recognised leaders, for example, Alice Bailey. But not everyone in the NAM would fully agree with everything that normally goes under that name.

The NAM is spreading and attracting many people, especially the young. Having started mainly in the U.S.A., it is increasingly an international movement. They see themselves as the people of the future, destined to take over the whole world. Many idealists are attracted to the movement because of its special concern for the environment and ecology - people may join "to save the planet" - and because of its belief in a one-world government to bring peace to mankind. The NAM would not normally describe itself as a religion - it would claim to embody the good elements in every religion. They see themselves as the true spiritual way for the future, and because of this claim they attract some people who are disillusioned with the materialism of much modern life.

Some Catholics and other Christians are trying to combine the New Age and Christianity. Certainly

Christians can share with the NAM such things as a concern for the environment and for peace. But there are a number of important elements in the NAM which are diametrically opposed to orthodox Christianity, and it is most important that Christians should be aware of these differences. There is a real danger of a woolly fuzziness which ends by sacrificing important elements of the Christian gospel.

Let us look at some of the elements of the NAM which are clearly not compatible with orthodox Christianity.

1. Astrology. The Age of Aquarius

Astrology plays an important part for many in the NAM. The New Age which we are entering into is the astrological era of Aquarius. About every 2100 years a different sign of the Zodiac is said to be in the ascendancy. The period from 2200 B.C. to the year 100 B.C. was said to be the Age of Aries - symbolised by the Ram - the time of Abraham and the Fatherhood of God. Then, coinciding with the Incarnation, came the Age of Pisces - symbolised by the Fish - an age centred on Jesus the Son. Now we are approaching the year 2000 A.D., which sees the dawning of the Age of Aquarius - symbolised by the Water Carrier - the age of the Spirit and liberated mankind.

So we are said to be moving into a new dispensation, rather like the New Testament period is for a Christian a different dispensation from the Old Testament period. It is not just a matter of a new historical era like, for example, the end of the Middle Ages. We are, it is claimed, moving into a very different period of human existence.

2. Jesus is not the Unique Saviour

It may have been all right to think of Jesus as the unique Saviour of mankind - which of course all orthodox Christians do - during the age of Pisces, but that no longer goes in the age of Aquarius. Jesus, like Buddha, is esteemed as one of the great teachers of mankind, but not the unique mediator between God and humankind. Moreover, many people in the NAM believe that a new Messiah will be born for the Age of Aquarius.

In NAM writings you will sometimes find references to Christ, but their Christ may not be the historical Jesus. An Anglican priest very drawn to the NAM complains in his book of "those churches which substitute a Jesus personality cult for the New Testament experience of the indwelling Christ, and who like Mary Magdalen need to let Jesus go in order to acquire that greater vision to which he is the supreme pointer." I have to admit that I find such statements very worrying. God forbid that Christians should ever give up their "Jesus personality cult" and "let Jesus go."

3. Pantheism

Another difficulty for an orthodox Christian is the blurring of the distinction between the Creator and the creation in the direction of pantheism. Our planet is seen as a living organism, Gaia. As one writer put it: "We now recognise the Earth as a single self-creating being that came alive in its whirling dance through space." This living earth, Gaia, is a kind of goddess. (I am all in favour of Christians giving greater prominence to the feminine element in religion and society but the NAM seem sometimes to believe not in the equality of the sexes but in the superiority of the female sex.)

4. Reincarnation

Belief in reincarnation is very widespread among those in the NAM. And this is clearly a major difference between orthodox Christianity and the NAM. Is our present life on this earth a unique happening - "It is appointed for mortals to die once, and after that the judgement" (Hebrews 9:27) - or is this one of many lives, perhaps hundreds and thousands? In the latter case, perhaps it does not matter much if we make a mess of things in this life, because there will be many other opportunities of putting things right.

Not a few people are being upset by New Age teaching on reincarnation. A woman came to me in great distress because she had been told by a New Age medium that she was a reincarnation of St. Teresa of Avila and of Mary, the mother of Jesus, and that she herself was going to be one of the major guru healers in the world. A widely recognised New Age leader had corrected the reincarnation of Mary message to a "partial reincarnation of Mary" - whatever that may be supposed to mean. The woman who came to me was profoundly upset by all this; and it took quite a time to calm her down. (Now, thank God, she has cut all links with the NAM and is a devout practicing Anglican.)

A man of 75 living in a seaside town was very upset

when informed by a NAM medium that his mother was now reincarnated and that if he met someone in the local town who attracted him, that was his mother.

It has been pointed out that very frequently people were said to have been outstanding personalities or to have occupied important positions in previous incarnations. It seems that mediums are more likely to reveal that you had been royalty, or an aristocrat, or an Egyptian Priestess, or an important composer, than that you had been a tin miner in Cornwall. Glory from the past can help to relieve present drabness!

New Age healers can, so they claim, help people to get in touch with their past lives experiences and this can, they say, be very important for healing present difficulties and for growth in this life. I even heard of one person with an international ministry who specialised in this method of healing. A Catholic man came to me to ask what he should do because his osteopath, whom he had found helpful, was now talking to him about the influence of his past incarnations on his present health problems. I suggested that he should look for an osteopath who was not into reincarnation.

As can be imagined, attributing past incarnations to oneself (or other people) provides a most fertile soil for fantasy. And this fantasy is increased considerably because the past incarnations can have been on other planets and galaxies. Someone can think, as one New Age leader did, that they were sent from another, more advanced, galaxy to help this earth to move into the New Age of Aquarius. The following quotation from a New Age paper gives some idea of what we are dealing with: "The predictions of ascension have come mainly from an organisation called the Great White Brotherhood, operating from the fifth dimension. Many members of the Great White Brotherhood have taken repeated incarnations on Earth as leaders, teachers, and healers and are known amongst their peers by different names to those by which they were known on Earth. The most notable amongst them, Sananda, came as Jesus the Christ. Kuthumi had more than one incarnation. He walked the earth as Pythagoras, John the Divine, and Francis of Assisi".

5. Spiritualism - Channelling

Spiritualism, which they usually refer to as channelling, is very widespread in the NAM. For example, the actress Shirley McLaine and a popular New Age channeller, J.Z. Knight, both claim that a 35,000 year old warrior called Ramtha communicates through them. Channelling, being a medium, in the NAM is not regarded as something just for a few people. Everyone is encouraged to learn to be a channeller, though some people will be specially gifted in his field.

For many in the NAM, channelling also provides a link between ourselves and the hundreds or thousands of UFOs which are, it is claimed, involved in helping our earth to move into the New Age of Aquarius. In some cases, higher entities, claiming to be extra-terrestrials, are said to pass on information from UFOs to the earth. "Flying saucers come mainly from Mars and Venus as per direct orders from Interplanetary Parliament. The seat of Interplanetary Parliament is

Saturn." In all this there is much human fantasising; and doubtless, not infrequently, demonic intervention.

6. Witchcraft and Paganism

In 1991 the NAM put on a series of TV Channel Four programmes and produced the book, 'The New Age. An Anthology of Essential Writings', edited by William Bloom (a Channel Four book). One of the contributors was Starhawk, described as "a white witch and the most influential New Age exponent on the religion and techniques of the Goddess and Wiccan" ('Wiccan' is an old English word for witchcraft). In her chapter Starhawk commends the values of witchcraft, for example: "Witchcraft offers the model of a religion of poetry, not theology".

So witchcraft is regarded as all right by many in the NAM. And linked with this is the attempt to revive Paganism and affirm the pre-Christian religions. Hence their special interest in places like Stonehenge, and the recommendation to practice magic. All this, needless to say, can easily open people up to demonic forces, as explained earlier in this book.

7. Psychic Knowledge, Healing, and Power.

It is part of New Age teaching that ordinary people can develop psychic gifts of knowledge, healing, and power over other people. Indeed, people should be encouraged and trained to develop these powers. And linked with this are the courses laid on to make business men and others more successful, like the Silva Mind Control courses. Some American firms expect their executives to follow such courses.

When people try to develop psychic knowleag and powers for worldly and selfish reasons, then the devil can very easily enter in. The promises of the NAM can seem very attractive, but it can easily all end in disaster.

Many New Age people are practitioners or supporters of the various alternative therapies or complimentary therapies which are increasingly attracting people today - therapies like osteopathy, acupuncture, reflexology, aroma-therapy, and homeopathy. As a result of this New Age involvement in these therapies, some Christians are simply describing these therapies as 'New Age' - this being understood as a condemnation. I think it is a great mistake simply to identify these therapies with the NAM. There are many good Christians who practice one or other of these therapies who would never in any way accept the New Age beliefs which I have mentioned above under six headings. So it is a very grave injustice to describe a Christian osteopath or acupuncturist or reflexologist as a New Ager. I met a very devout young Catholic woman who trained as a homeopathic therapist after her mother had been significantly helped by homeopathy. This fervent Catholic was understandably hurt when she met Christians who regarded what she was doing as New Age and demonic.

I myself seek healing through Christian prayer ministry and through the medical profession. I do not go to practitioners of alternative therapies. But I am particularly fortunate in being able to receive ministry from many Christians in the healing ministry of prayer. I would have no objection in principle to receiving ministry from, say, a Christian osteopath or acupuncturist. The priest who is probably the best-known Catholic exorcist in the world, because of his exceptionally powerful gift of casting out devils, told me that he had received acupuncture treatment from a good Christian. I know several very discerning Catholics in the healing and deliverance ministry who seek healing from practitioners of the alternative therapies. I know a priest truly gifted in healing and deliverance who told me of two Catholics professionally involved in acupuncture who send him some of their clients for prayer ministry - and he is quite happy with the ministry of the acupuncturists. I have talked with two prayerful Catholic religious sisters who are trained as reflexologists, and I have no reason to feel unhappy about their therapy. (They also both pray for the healing of their clients.)

Does all this mean that I am happy for anyone to go to any of the practitioners of the alternative therapies? Definitely, No! Those Christians who warn us about certain dangers here have their reasons. Some things like spiritualist healing are always wrong. But therapies like acupuncture or osteopathy can be all right if the therapist is a sound person. If the therapist is a good Christian or a person of moral and spiritual integrity, then the therapy could be helpful. But if the therapist is into the occult or witchcraft, then the client could pick up negative spiritual influences from the therapist, could indeed pick up demonic forces, even if at another level they had received some healing. And we must face the fact that there are not a few alternative therapists who are involved in the occult or witchcraft.

So we have to discern not only about the soundness of the therapy, but also and often especially, about the therapist. Is he or she a good Christian or a person of spiritual and moral integrity? Is he or she open to or involved in the occult or witchcraft? Discernment of this kind is not always easy. We have to rely both on prayer and the recommendations of sound people. It might be simpler if we could say that this therapy is always O.K. or never O.K. But the reality of life is often more complex. If we say that the therapy is always O.K., then some people may pick up evil influences from unsound therapists. If we say that the therapy is never O.K., then some people may fail to receive the healing God wanted them to receive from that therapy. (I know a Catholic man who had a very painful sickness of the neck. Because of the pain he had to give up his work. He spent much time - and much of his savings - seeking healing from the medical profession and from Christians involved in the healing ministry of prayer, both Catholics and Evangelicals. All apparently to no avail. Finally he tried Shiatsu therapy, a sort of Japanese physiotherapy, and this resulted in a big reduction in the pain, so that he can now work again as a university lecturer: and his spiritual life has, I think, also benefited from the relief of pain. If he had been told that all Shiatsu was evil and that as a Christian he should have nothing to do with it, then he might well still be in his great pain.)

The differing attitude of Christians towards the alternative therapies can be affected by divergent theologies. Catholics and Evangelicals agree that no one is saved except by Jesus: "I am the way, and the truth, and the life. No one comes to the Father except through me." (John 14:6). However, Catholics, and many other Christians, believe that Jesus is saving many good people who do not call themselves Christians - indeed, who may never have even heard of the name of Jesus, while some Evangelicals believe that only people with an explicit conscious faith in Jesus are on the way of salvation. Catholics believe that God is at work in religions like Islam, Hinduism, and Buddhism, while some Evangelicals believe that these religions are simply of the devil. Catholics believe that God is at work in many other areas of life which are not explicitly Christian, while some evangelicals would seem to deny this.

What has this to do with the alternative therapies? Some Evangelicals would say that those therapies which came from pagan religious backgrounds or simply non-Christian backgrounds, must be demonic because of the source from which they come. Thus acupuncture must be demonic because it comes from a demonic Chinese pagan background. Catholics would believe than since God is at work in Chinese religion, then he can also be at work in acupuncture, though the acupuncture may sometimes have to be purified or cleansed from some of its pagan associations.

The inter-faith dialogue is another area where there can be disagreements. While insisting strongly on

Jesus as the unique Saviour of the human race, the Catholic Church believes in dialoguing and co-operating with religions like Islam, Hinduism, and Buddhism. At Assisi, Pope John Paul II asked leaders of other religions to pray for peace with him, each in their own way. Some Evangelicals regarded this as trying to co-operate with the devil.

The Catholic attitude is seen in the following two quotations, one from Vatican II and one from Pope John Paul II:

"Different religions have tried to respond to mankind's search for the ultimate explanation of creation and the meaning of man's journey through life. The Catholic Church accepts the truth and goodness found in these religions and she sees reflections there of the truth of Christ, whom she proclaims as 'the Way, the Truth, and the Life'. She wishes to do everything possible to co-operate with other believers in preserving all that is good in their religions and cultures, stressing the things that are held in common and helping all people to live as brothers and sisters." (Vatican II, Nostra Aetate, nn.1-3)

"The Catholic Church is endeavouring to engage in friendly dialogue with all the great religions that have guided mankind throughout history. This we shall continue to do, so that our mutual understanding and collaboration may increase, and so that the spiritual and moral values we uphold may continue to offer wisdom and inner strength to the men and women of our time." (Pope John Paul II, Seoul, 6th May 1984)

Some of the Evangelicals with whom I would disagree about alternative therapies and inter-faith dialogue are very wonderful Christians, great evangelists, and have very powerful healing ministries. I thank God for them and for their ministries, but I know where I, as a Catholic, disagree with them. Apart from the difference mentioned above, if they tell me that I should not ask Our Lady to pray for me, I do not follow them. I thank God for their great love for Jesus, which is central, but I continue also to ask Our Lady to pray for me.

I think that some Catholics can be so impressed by the evangelism and healing ministry of certain Evangelicals that they are over-influenced by some of these Evangelicals' ideas - ideas which are not fully Catholic. So that these Catholics can start condemning, for example, all alternative therapies and all inter-faith dialogue as being demonic.

Catholics, however, can also be put off all inter-faith dialogue because not a few Christians, including some Catholics, who are enthusiastic for or support the inter-faith dialogue do in fact exaggerate and compromise with important Christian truths. For example, one Catholic priest wrote in a book: "Since living beings are not static but always moving through cycles of birth, growth, maturity, and in the case of human beings ***re-birth*** (my emphasis), change is a fundamental quality of life". He also wrote: "The other indication that the New Age of Consciousness is coming to fruition in our time, comes from the field of astrology. This accounts for the fact that the emerging

New Age is often referred to as the Age of Aquarius". There is a considerable amount of Hindu influence in the NAM and Hindus, of course, believe in reincarnation and astrology. But these are not permissible options for orthodox Christians.

Here is a final quotation from this priest: "Before 6th August 1945 we had understood God to be the sole creator and sustainer of human life and implicit in that was the belief that he was the sole terminator of life as a whole. We have now assumed this power for ourselves. We co-create with God by allowing life to continue. We now share the mastery over the life of our world with God. God is no long 'Almighty God'. God can no longer be understood as being externally related to the world as the power that totally controls it". So the "We believe in one God, the Father, the ***Almighty***, maker of heaven and earth" of the Creed has disappeared.

No wonder that some Christians feel that if this is the result of inter-faith dialogue, then they want to have nothing to do with it. However, alongside an irresponsible inter-faith dialogue there is a responsible one, such as that conducted by the Vatican. I would urge Catholics and other Christians not to turn away from this kind of authentic dialogue and co-operation on account of the irresponsible one.

There are also questions of pastoral prudence and wisdom when it comes to inter-faith dialogue and co-operation. It is one thing for a committed Christian with a firm faith to study other religions and dialogue with them - that can be a very good thing. It is something else for a Christian with a wobbly faith to do so - and there are many Christians in this country whose faith is very wobbly when it comes to things like believing that Jesus is the only Saviour. For such Christians inter-faith dialogue and gatherings can easily become the road to becoming, say, a Buddhist. Now I am not sending to hell every baptised Christian who becomes a Buddhist! But I would think that every believing Christian should be unhappy when Christians become Buddhists. For believing Christians, Christianity and Buddhism are not two equal religions. Christ is the unique Saviour of the world, Buddha is not. It is very easy for some inter-faith language and practice to give the impression that we all regard one religion as good as another. I think that inter-faith dialogue and co-operation require a pastoral prudence and wisdom which they do not always receive.

Pope John Paul II, who was such a strong opponent of communism, has pointed out that not everything in communism was evil. Similarly, not everything in the NAM is evil. It has been necessary in this chapter to state clearly the elements in the NAM which are mistaken or wrong. But everything in the NAM is not evil.

I think that their concern for the environment and for ecologically 'saving the planet' are the most important positive elements. And many Christians could sometimes learn from the example of the NAM in this field. New Age people tend to be kind to animals. They are often wise on the subject of diet -

which does not mean that we all have to become vegetarians. They also often adopt a helpful holistic approach to health. Some Christians find New Age music helpful and something for which they can thank God. And New Age people do not fall into the pitfalls of a narrow nationalism, which has caused so many wars. So all is not negative in the NAM, and we can appreciate and thank God for the positive elements.

There is in our Christian tradition an authentic strand which is very appreciative of the beauty of nature and is deeply aware of God's presence in nature. It is also strongly conscious of our links with the natural world. St. Francis of Assisi is an outstanding example of this spiritual strand, with his love for animals and nature. In his Canticle of Brother Sun, he writes of Sisters Moon and Stars, of Brothers Wind and Air, of Sister Water, of Brother Fire, of Sister Earth our Mother, and of Sister Death. Many saints, for example St. Hildegard, were very aware of the presence of God in the natural beauty of the world. A good number of the psalms and canticles call upon the natural world to praise God, for example, in Psalm 148 we read: "Praise the Lord from the earth, you sea monsters and all deeps, fire and hail, snow and frost, stormy wind fulfiling his command! Mountains and all hills, fruit trees and all cedars! Wild animals and all cattle, creeping things and flying birds .... Let them praise the name of the Lord, for his name alone is exalted, his glory is above earth and heaven." I myself find the beauty of flowers and nature a great help to prayer. I think that if we developed more this strand of Christian spirituality, then fewer Christians would feel drawn to the NAM.

There is a book which I would strongly recommend people interested in the NAM to read: 'Inside the New Age Nightmare', by Randall N. Baer (Huntingdon House, U.S.A.). The author was fully involved in the NAM for 15 years, and had become a well-known leader and author in the movement in the U.S.A. Then he had a vision of "demons filled with the power of Satan", and this led to a profound conversion to Christianity, helped by the tele-evangelists. He now spends his life trying to convert New Agers to Christianity.

In his book he shows how sincere he was in his New Age beliefs until he had the vision of demons. He really did believe in the New Age fantasies, including the belief that he himself originally came from another galaxy. Looking back he sees himself as having been deceived by the devil. I would agree with him that there is much demonic deception in the New Age. However, I cannot say that I share his conviction that the New Age is soon to usher in the final Antichrist prior to the Second Coming of Jesus.

It seems to me that in the subjects treated in this chapter, Christians need to seek a balanced middle road. Some Christians see no harm in the NAM, others see nothing but the devil in it. Some Christians see no danger in alternative therapies whoever the therapist is, others regard them all as totally demonic. Some Christians happily embrace every form of inter-faith activity, others refuse all co-operation with other religions. And the excesses in one direction tend to re-inforce the excesses in the other. Let us seek to be balanced in our understanding and activity. Having said that, however, I think that every convinced Christian should deeply regret the spreading of the NAM, a movement which in so many ways is contrary to the Christian Gospel.

I would especially ask those Catholics who are aware of the demonic dangers not to exaggerate. If they do they will cause other Catholics simply to dismiss them as having been brain-washed by extreme Evangelicals, with the result that these other Catholics will not listen to the true warnings they need to hear from them. For example, if many Catholics are told by you that anyone who has been to any osteopath or homeopathic practitioner needs to be exorcised then, especially if they have been helped by an osteopath or homeopathy, they will regard you as a nut case and not listen to your warning that therapy from someone involved in the occult or a witch can be dangerous.

In the whole subject of this chapter - indeed of this book - we very much need to be led by the light of the Holy Spirit. None of us has all the answers about everything. May I suggest that the reader now pauses for a time of prayer to the Holy Spirit, asking that he or she be enlightened and guided by the Holy Spirit.

Chapter Five

Countering the Attacks of the Devil

1. Concentrating on Jesus and on Holiness

The best way in general for a Christian to fight against the attacks and work of the devil is not to think about him too much, but to concentrate on Jesus and on living by the grace of God a positive Christian life. As we seek to grow in faith, hope, love, and humility; as we seek to grow in holiness, then we shall by so doing be defending ourselves against the attacks of the devil. It is Jesus not the devil who must occupy our thoughts; it is the love of Jesus, not our concern for the devil which must motivate and inspire our lives.

We should know that the devil and demons exist; we should know which are the paths they are trying to lead us down; we should learn to recognise their presence and their attacks both on ourselves and others; we should know how to counter their attacks and their work; but our habitual focus should be very much on Jesus and the things of Jesus.

2. The Importance of Prayer and the Sacraments

Developing a deep life of prayer is very important for our spiritual warfare. A Christian with a weak life of prayer cannot expect to be able to cope with the "wiles of the devil" (Ephesians 6:11). A serious life of prayer means giving enough time to it; it means prayerfully reading the Bible. It means for Catholics as far as we can making good use of the sacraments, especially of the Holy Eucharist. Receiving Our Lord daily, or as frequently as possible, in communion, can be a wonderful protection against demonic attacks. And there is still a place for praying before the Blessed Sacrament. We should not under-estimate the power of Jesus in the Eucharist to protect, to heal, and to liberate. Going to confession helps many Catholics in their spiritual warfare. The comparative neglect of this sacrament by many Catholics is something to be regretted. Regular confession can help to keep the enemy out.

3. Praise

The release of praise in a Christian's life can be very important for spiritual warfare. The devil hates people praising God, praising Jesus. The praise of Jesus can sometimes be enough to drive demonic forces from a person or from a place - this has been the experience of the Charismatic Renewal. Sometimes also people are healed through the prayer of intense praise. (The devil can play his part in causing not only spiritual and emotional sickness, but also physical sickness.) So become more and more a man or woman of praise if you want to keep the devil away.

4. Repentance

Growth in repentance can be very important for spiritual warfare. When we humble ourselves in repentance, the devil can find he has lost his foothold. His flaming darts cannot strike home when someone is humble and repentant. Our pride gives him the opportunity of causing trouble.

We all need to grow in repentance every day. Original sin goes deep in each one of us. As the years go by, I become more aware of areas of my life where repentance is needed. Let us ask the Holy Spirit to give us a greater spirit of repentance, to show us what are the things we need to repent of. As we grow in repentance and humility we will find that we are increasingly protected from the attacks of the devil.

5. Deliberate Sin

Deliberate, repeated sin which is not repented of, gives demons the opportunity to get a grip on people. Thus deliberate and repeated seriously excessive drinking will allow an evil spirit of alcoholic addition to enter, and deliberate and repeated turning to pornography will allow an evil spirit of lust to get in. Other examples could be given which would let in evil spirits of pride, anger, violence, suicide, blasphemy, jealousy, homosexuality, lesbianism, greed, fear, and laziness - and the list could be extended.

6. The Devil and Demons

Should we think in terms of attacks by the devil or by more than one demon? Certainly the New Testament speaks of more than one demon: the devil or Satan being the leader. Is it right to give them names, such as those mentioned above? Many experienced exorcists seem to find some naming helpful. However, this naming can be exaggerated, as also the number of demons claimed to have been cast out of a person. Yet we remember that in the New Testament seven demons were said to have been cast out of Mary Magdalene (Mark 16:9), and in Mark chapter 5 the reply to the question of Jesus was: "My name is Legion; for we are many" (verse 9). The New Testament also mentions "unclean" spirits (e.g. Luke 9:42 and 11:24) and a "spirit of infirmity" (Luke 13:11), as also "a demon that was mute" (Luke 11:14). Then there is the evil spirit who "goes and brings seven other spirits more evil than itself, and they enter and live there, and the last state of that person is worse than the first" (Luke 11:26). However, I would not wish to be too dogmatic about names and numbers of demons. The basic truth is that the devil and his demons exist and that they attack human beings.

7. Prayer to Our Lady

Many Catholics have found that prayer to Our Lady has been very effective against demonic forces. The devil seems particularly to attack some people when they are dying, and the custom of saying the Hail Mary will mean that we have especially asked her to pray for us "at the hour of our death". (Incidentally, I sometimes wonder whether it would not be better to change the prayer to "the time of our death", for the period of dying can be a very long hour, indeed extending for many days. "Time of our death" would cover the relevant period, whether it was shorter or longer.) Not a few people find it helpful to say the Rosary when they feel under demonic attack. Although Jesus should always have very much the first place in our prayers, we will be wise not to forget his mother. Catholics who more or less miss out on prayer to Mary are neglecting a powerful source of help.

8. Holy Scripture

The use of passages or phrases from the Bible can be a great help in spiritual warfare, for the Word of God in Holy Scripture has a special power of its own. For example, at a time when we feel that we are under special demonic attack, we can read the psalm: "The Lord is my shepherd, I shall not want" (psalm 23/22). Or we may prefer the Compline psalm 91/90, where we say: "For he will deliver you from the snare of the fowler and from the deadly pestilence.... You will not fear the terror of the night, or the arrow that flies by day, or the pestilence that stalks in the darkness."

We may find it helpful to call out with the tax collector: "God, be merciful to me a sinner!" (Luke 18:13). Or to say with Our Lady: "Here am I, the servant of the Lord; let it be with me according to your word" (Luke 1:38). Other helpful New Testament texts may be Matthew 10:29, about "the hairs of your head", and Matthew 11:28, which starts with: "Come to me, all you that are weary and are carrying heavy burdens, and I will give you rest."

9. The Our Father

The Our Father, the prayer which Jesus himself taught us, is of course suitable for all occasions. The habit of saying it slowly and prayerfully can be a great blessing. The last line is particularly applicable to spiritual warfare: "but rescue us from the evil one", as the N.R.S.V. translates it. Some translations just have "evil", but it seems that the early Christians understood "evil one" there. In any case, "evil" includes demonic evil.

10. The Good Angels

As suggested earlier in this book, we should not neglect the role of the good angels in spiritual warfare. According to Catholic tradition, we each have a guardian angel at our side to help us and protect us. This is indeed a wonderful gift, and it is a pity that Christians do not reflect more on this. Just think about it! You have always with you an angel sent by God to help and protect you. The angel is there when you are awake and when you are sleeping. He is at your side when danger arises - spiritual danger, physical danger, danger from illness. He is with you helping when you are doing or seeking to do something important for God's kingdom. He is next to you when you are being good and when you are sinning.

So ought we not to be thanking him and asking for his protection much more than we normally do? For decades I had the habit of saying a short prayer at night - if I had not fallen asleep first - to ask my guardian angel for his protection. But it was a very short prayer, said without much sense of conviction. In recent times the reality and presence of my guardian angel has increasingly meant more to me. So I not only ask him for his protection - and with greater confidence now - but I also thank him. How ungrateful I have been in not thanking him in the past! It is only when, by the grace of God, we get to heaven that we shall learn how much our guardian angel has done for us during our life, how many scrapes he has saved us from. And nowadays I not only pray to my guardian angel at night, but on other occasions, for instance if I set out on a journey or have to minister to a disturbed person. Indeed, I find myself sometimes just chatting to my guardian angel!

Let us not forget the words of psalm 91/90: "For he will command his angels concerning you, to guard you in all your ways. On their hands they will bear you up, so that you will not dash your foot against a stone."

I may add that I also say daily the following payer to St. Michael, which we used to say after every Mass: "Holy Michael, Archangel, defend us in the day of battle; be our safeguard against the wickedness and snares of the devil. May God rebuke him, we humbly pray; and do thou, prince of the heavenly host, by the power of God thrust down to hell Satan, and all wicked spirits who wander through the world for the ruin of souls. Amen." I know well not a few Catholics who find it helpful to say this prayer daily, and especially when the situation is or might be dangerous.

11. Christian Community

If in our spiritual warfare we seek the support of angels and saints, we should also seek help from living people, especially other Christians. We are members of the Body of Christ and we journey towards heaven not as isolated people but as members of the Christian family. When climbers are in dangerous situations they are often linked to each other by a rope, so that if one falls the others can hold him or her up. So it should be with Christians. Faced with the dangers of life we need to be roped to others, so that if we fall the others can hold us up; so that if one person is being strongly attacked by the devil other members of the Christian family are there to support.

I think that one of the weaknesses of much parish life is that many parishioners are far too isolated; that they do not have adequate support from other Christians; that there is a lack of community. One of the advantages of living in a monastery is that one has the loving and caring support of other brethren. The charismatic prayer group and other similar groups help to provide loving fellowship, which is a great help for Christians in their spiritual warfare. For me it has been a wonderful experience to be upheld by the loving prayers and help of so many brothers and sisters in the Charismatic Renewal, not least in my healing ministry and in the writing of this book.

The clergy of course have a special role in building community; in helping Christians in their needs. However, it should not all be left to the clergy, who in any case are far too few in number to be able to cope with all the needy people. Every Christian is called to support other people in their Christian walk, and this includes the countering of demonic attacks.

12. Spiritual Counsellors

I think every Christian should if possible have a spiritual counsellor - I prefer this word counsellor to director, for director sounds rather authoritarian, and in one sense only the Holy Spirit should be our director.

The spiritual counsellor can be important from the point of view of spiritual warfare. The devil is very cunning and subtle in the ways he tempts and attacks us, and he sometimes disguises himself as an "angel of light" (2 Corinthians 11:14). We can easily be deceived. If we are in the habit of revealing everything - including the most humiliating and shameful actions and temptations - to a spiritual counsellor, then the devil is less likely to be able to deceive us. A wise and prayerful spiritual counsellor will sometimes be able to see things more objectively than we can. The spiritual counsellor does not have to be a priest - most priests simply have not the time for much ministry of this kind. In any case, some lay people are more gifted in this ministry than many priests - think of a St. Catherine of Siena.

13. The Armour of God

An increasing number of Christians, especially in the Charismatic Renewal, are finding it helpful in their spiritual warfare to put on the armour of God. This practice is based on the passage in Ephesians chapter 6 quoted earlier. There St. Paul tells Christians to "take up the whole armour of God" (verse 13), and he then proceeds to mention the various pieces of armour, the belt of truth, the breastplate of righteousness, the shoes to proclaim the gospel of peace, the shield of faith, the helmet of salvation, and the sword of the Spirit. (I personally put on the armour of God every morning and night, and occasionally before situations which may be especially difficult. But it is important not to do it too often - that would be concentrating too much on the dangers, and the enemy, and not trusting Jesus enough.)

There is no one formula for putting on the armour of God, indeed I think the prayers should be to some extent adapted to the needs of each person. The formula produced below has been found helpful by some people. Things like anger, unforgiveness, lust, jealousy, should be slipped in if they are proving difficult. It is customary to make the appropriate physical gestures as the prayers are said, for example, placing the hands on the head when putting on the helmet of salvation.

PUTTING ON THE ARMOUR OF GOD

1. I place upon my HEAD the HELMET OF SALVATION as a protection against all thinking, speaking, seeing, hearing, feeling, which is not of you.

2. I place upon my CHEST the BREASTPLATE OF RIGHTEOUSNESS as a protection against all unrighteous thoughts, all fear and anxiety, all sickness and all harm to the body.

3. I place round my WAIST the GIRDLE OF TRUTH that I may be truthful at every level of my being.

4. I place on my FEET the SANDALS OF THE GOSPEL OF PEACE that I may be the messenger of your GOOD NEWS to others.

5. I take in my LEFT HAND the SHIELD OF FAITH with which to quench all the flaming darts of the enemy.

6. I take in my RIGHT HAND the SWORD OF THE SPIRIT with which to attack the strongholds of the enemy.

(Ephesians 6:11-17)

14. The Sign of the Cross

Traditionally, Catholics are accustomed to making the sign of the Cross, especially perhaps in times of danger. When we make the sign of the Cross we are thinking both of the Blessed Trinity and of the Cross of Jesus. We can call on Jesus to protect us by the power of his Cross.

It should be added that exorcists often make the sign of the Cross over people when they are seeking to deliver them from evil spirits. And people and objects are blessed by making the sign of the Cross over them.

15. Holy Water, Crucifixes, Holy Pictures, Medals

Sacramentals have their place in aiding us in our spiritual warfare. I think it is a pity that more Catholics do not make use of Holy Water, which traditionally was used for protection against demonic forces. It is surely good to have crucifixes in evidence in a home, and I personally like always to have a crucifix with me. Again, the crucifix is traditionally linked with spiritual warfare. In solemn exorcism, the exorcist makes use of the crucifix.

Icons, pictures, and statues of the saints - and especially of Our Lady - can be an inspiration in the Christian life and a real help in spiritual warfare. When I was ill recently a Divine Mercy picture of Jesus and an icon of Our Lady were a very real help to me. Holy pictures and crucifixes can aid us in concentrating our thoughts on the things of God when the enemy is attacking us.

Then there are holy medals and scapulars, and the practice of lighting candles. Again, many Catholics find them to be truly helpful. The blessing for the medal of St. Benedict includes the prayer: "O almighty God, giver of all good things, we humbly beseech you that through the intercession of St. Benedict you would pour forth your blessing upon these medals so that all who shall wear them and earnestly strive to perform good works, may deserve to obtain health of soul and body, the grace of increasing holiness, and that they may strive by the help of your mercy to escape all the snares and deceits of the devil, and thus be able to appear holy and stainless in your sight. Amen."

Warnings

At the end of this chapter two warnings are necessary. First, we are protected from the attacks of the devil and misfortunes, not by a relic, a crucifix, a holy picture, a medal, a scapular, a particular prayer, but by Jesus himself. He may choose to work through an angel or in answer to the prayers of his mother or the saints, or through pious objects, but it is Jesus himself who saves and protects. There can be a danger of superstition as also of a magic mentality if we put our trust in holy things rather than in the Holy One.

The second warning is that there can be a danger of some Catholics getting smothered by a multitude of private devotions, special prayers, novenas, holy pictures, scapulars, medals and such things, so that the centrality of the Mass and the basic simplicity of the spiritual life become obscured. And we should remember that we shall not be protected from the attacks of the devil because of the vast number of pious objects around us, or because of endless private devotions. We need to be discerning in our use of holy objects and holy practices. However, I think far more Catholics are now in danger of neglecting these things than of over-doing them.

Finally, may I invite the reader at the end of this chapter to spend some time in silent prayer. Ask the Holy Spirit to show you what, if anything, God wants you to do about the things mentioned in this chapter. Maybe you are already doing all that God is asking of you. Fine. But there may be some things God wants you to take note of; there may be some suggestions in this chapter which are for you.

Come Holy Spirit !

Chapter Six

Rebuking Evil Spirits and Offensive Spiritual Warfare

"He called the twelve and began to send them out two by two, and gave them authority over the unclean spirits..... So they went out and proclaimed that all should repent. They cast out many demons, and anointed with oil many who were sick and cured them" (Mark 6:7).

"And these signs will accompany those who believe; by using my name they will cast out demons" (Mark 16:17).

The Catholic Church - and other churches also - has always had a ministry of casting out demons, in accordance with the words of Jesus quoted above. Indeed for many centuries there was a special office of exorcist to which people were ordained.

According to the present discipline of the Catholic Church, solemn exorcism of the possessed is reserved to priests who have received permission from the bishop for this ministry and there should be co-operation with the medical profession if possible (Canon 1172). However, lesser forms of deliverance prayer are permitted to Catholics, indeed we all pray for deliverance whenever we say the Our Father: "But deliver us from evil". (The new Catholic Catechism comments: "In this petition, evil is not an abstraction, but refers to a person, Satan, the Evil One, the angel who opposes God" (2851).)

So an ordinary Catholic may not perform solemn exorcisms of the possessed; may not directly command an evil spirit in the name of Jesus to leave a possessed person (imprecatory prayer). Nor may they command an evil spirit in a possessed person to reveal its name. However, an ordinary Catholic may ask Jesus to deliver someone from the devil or an evil spirit of, say, anger, lust, or fear. But such a prayer should not normally be said aloud in the presence of the person except after prayerful discernment, for obviously it could easily frighten and upset some people and do more harm than good. Father James McManus CSSR in his very excellent book, 'Healing in the Spirit - Inner Healing and Deliverance in Today's Church' (DLT), rightly underlines the usefulness of silent prayers of exorcism and deliverance (page 114). Silent prayers have the advantage of not frightening people, either the needy person or others present. However, there obviously remains a place for a deliverance prayer spoken aloud - Jesus to our knowledge did not exorcise people silently, and the official Roman Ritual assumes that the exorcism prayers will normally be said aloud. If someone is feeling that they are being tormented by evil spirits, then they will usually be very glad to hear someone praying aloud against the evil spirits.

When praying in someone's presence for their deliverance from evil spirits it would be good to proceed in the following way:

1. Start with the prayer of praise, and intermingle praise with the rest of the prayer. Praising Jesus is powerful.
2. Pray for the protection of everyone present. For example, one could pray: "Jesus, through your Precious Blood, protect John and all of us present from all harm, evil, and attacks of the devil. Amen." One could also ask Our Lady, the saints, and the angels to protect with their prayer all present. The prayer to Holy Michael, Archangel, would be appropriate.
3. Ask Jesus to bind any evil spirits in the person who is being payed for. For example: "Jesus, please bind any evil spirits in John." Or, "Jesus, please bind any evil spirit of fear or anger in John." (Exorcists have often found from experience that if they first 'bind' an evil spirit in the name of Jesus, then it will frequently be easier afterwards to cast out.)
4. Then ask Jesus to cast out any evil spirits from the person in question. For example, "Jesus, please cast out any evil spirits in John and command them not to return." Or, "Jesus, please cast out any evil spirit of fear in John and command it not to return."
5. Pray for the infilling of the Holy Spirit, for the departure of evil spirits can leave a vacuum, and one does not want them to return. For example: "Jesus, please fill John's whole being with your Holy Spirit, so that there is room in John for nothing which is not of you."

However, it needs to be said that cases of real possession should be referred to the Bishop or to an official exorcist. We also need to remember that while asking Jesus to liberate people from evil spirits of things like fear, depression, and infirmity is not normally dangerous, dealing with evil spirits of things like Satanism, witchcraft, and violence can be very dangerous. In this whole ministry people should know their limitations and not take on too much. It is better to remain on the side of caution. Praying a deprecatory prayer asking Jesus to cast out an evil spirit may not be against the present discipline of the Church, but it could often be very unwise.

Catholics can also rebuke the devil or demons if they feel that they themselves are being tempted or attacked by them. Thus Catholics who felt that they were being attacked could pray aloud, for example: "Devil (or evil spirit of anger, or lust, or fear, or witchcraft), in the name of Jesus Christ I bind you, I command you to leave me and to go to Jesus." Or a shorter prayer could be used, for example: "Devil, in the name of Jesus I command you to be gone!" Or they may prefer to use a deprecatory prayer, for example: "Jesus, please bind this evil spirit of hate and command it to leave me and not return". Or they may prefer simply to pray: "Jesus, have mercy on me, a sinner". The important thing is to pray as the Holy Spirit guides.

Not only people, but also places may be in need of a deliverance prayer of one kind or another. Not so infrequently people will complain that their home or part of their home or some other building seems to be disturbed in one way or another. It may be that a ghost is seen from time to time. It may be that footsteps are heard or the sound of knocking, when no human person was there. Perhaps there is a special coldness in part of the house which cannot be explained naturally. There may be unpleasant smells which cannot be accounted for. Quite often there will be inexplicable interference with electrical equipment. Also, things may move around in a room: for instance a woman told me that she would find articles like tea towels on top of a kitchen cabinet, when no member of the family or anyone else had put them there. A priest told me that once when he was blessing a home, a stationary golf ball suddenly and inexplicably shot across the room. Some of this may be referred to as poltergeist phenomena.

Disturbances like these may be due to various causes. Perhaps someone who had lived and died in the house is not at peace - the appearances or activity of a ghost could be a call for help, a call for prayer for the repose of their soul. Perhaps the troubles are due to the fact that someone living in the house, or who had lived in the house, is or was involved in some form of occult activity, for example spiritualism, witchcraft, or playing with ouija boards. Perhaps the disturbances are linked with acute personal tensions in one or more of the occupants of the house, especially adolescents.

Obviously in cases like these there is a special need to turn to prayer. Some years ago another priest, a religious sister, and I, were called in by the authorities of another diocese to help with a large public building where strange things were happening, and this was causing real problems. The caretaker would not go round the top corridor to turn off the lights in the evening on his own, because once he had seen a ghost there, and he had also once felt pushed from behind. In the office of the main administrator a picture kept falling off a wall in an inexplicable way - and it would be found on the floor in the middle of the room. There was a very unpleasant smell in the room at times, which building experts could not explain. And the room was sometimes very cold in an inexplicable way. The cleaning woman and others did not like going into the room. There was a third place in the building where strange things were happening: I forget what. We celebrated a requiem Mass in the administrator's office for the repose of the soul of anyone not at peace connected with the building. (The fairly new building had been built on an ancient grave yard.) We went round the parts of the building where strange things had been happening, casting out any evil spirits which may have been there, asking Jesus to fill the place with his healing presence, and continuing to pray for the repose of any departed people not at peace. We learned from the bishop a few years later that there had been no further problems with the building since our visit.

On another occasion three of us went to a very old rural house in the same diocese. The lady who lived there was frequently - about once a week - seeing a ghost appear in the living room. The ghost had the appearance of a man with a sad face, dressed in a style of clothing of some centuries ago. When the ghost appeared the dog would be upset. The ghost would disappear up by the wall next to the chimney. There were also two rooms in the house which felt exceptionally cold, and indeed the whole house had a rather unpleasant atmosphere.

We celebrated a requiem Mass for the repose of the soul of the ghost and of any other departed person not at peace who was linked with the house. We also went round blessing the whole house with holy water and casting out any evil spirits or forces which may have been present in the house. Three months later the lady of the house told me that there had been no more appearances of the ghost, that the cold places in the house were considerably less cold, and that the whole atmosphere of the house felt better.

I think it is reasonable to believe that in this last case, the appearances of the ghost were a call for help, and that after the Mass he was at peace and there was no reason to go on appearing. There were probably also, in my opinion, negative influences connected with evil spirits in the house, and the Mass together with the rebuking of evil spirits could have chased them away - the past cold areas probably pointed to the presence of evil spirits.

In the first case of the large public building, the requiem Mass may well have helped one or more departed souls and the casting out of evil spirits was probably also needed. I think that quite often we shall never know for certain whether disturbances were caused by departed souls or evil spirits or both. If, however, peace is restored to the building and to the people who live there, then our mission has been accomplished, whether or not we ever know what had been causing the disturbance. (Our mission may also have included ministering to the needs of the living.)

I think that what has been written above underlines the rightness of praying for homes and buildings, of getting a priest to come and bless them, and if possible to have a Mass celebrated there. These are good things to do whether or not there have been signs of disturbance in the house or building. In a house or building there can be a bad spiritual atmosphere, a neutral one, or a good one. Obviously, we should seek to have as good a spiritual atmosphere as possible. The spiritual tone of the people who now live in a building is normally the main creator of spiritual atmospheres, good or bad. But influences from the past can play their part, and sometimes very much so.

It should be added that some people are much more sensitive than others when it comes to being aware of the spiritual atmosphere of a place. I do not consider myself to be especially sensitive in this field, so I find it helpful when ministering in the ways described in this chapter to have with me someone more sensitive than myself. Some sensitive people will feel immediately that things are all right or not all right in this house or this room. However, judgements of that kind are never infallible. So it can sometimes be wise if possible to get another person gifted in this way to confirm the discernment. And we also need to use our Christian common sense in these matters.

(Readers who are interested in reading further in this field should see the two books of Dr. Kenneth McAll, an Anglican psychiatrist: 'Healing the Family Tree' (Sheldon Press) and 'Healing the Haunted' (Darley Anderson). Although Catholics may not agree with all the ideas of Kenneth McAll, I think he has been a key pioneer to whom we are greatly indebted.)

Our spiritual warfare should not only be defensive, but also offensive. As Derek Prince writes: "As long as Satan keeps the church on the defensive, his kingdom will never be overthrown. Therefore, we have an absolute obligation to move out from the defensive and from mere self-protection to an attack position" - 'Spiritual Warfare', page 98, (Derek Prince Ministries - International). And on page 99: "Jesus pictures the church on the offensive, attacking the gates of Satan. Jesus promises that Satan's gates will not hold out against the church and that Satan will not be able to keep the church out".

Whenever Christians pray authentically for peace and justice in the world, for the conversion of their country, for an end to abortions or drug addiction, for the feeding of the hungry, for the protection of the environment, for the saving of the crumbling marriage of their daughter, for the healing of their husband's alcoholism, then they are involved in spiritual warfare, whether they think in terms of spiritual warfare or not. Thus every prayerful celebration of Mass and every devout recitation of the Divine Office or the rosary is part of the spiritual battle.

However, sometimes Christians can feel called to engage in offensive spiritual warfare in a very conscious way. In the early seventies there was a Catholic Charismatic prayer group meeting weekly in the Soho area of London, which area especially during those years was known as a centre of sexual immorality. The prayer group felt called in a special way to pray against the immorality in the district.

Myles Dempsey, the leader of the group, who later founded the Prince of Peace Community, tells how during the prayer meetings some of its members would, in pairs, for a short time walk around the area, praying before immoral establishments. One evening they found that a new immoral establishment had been opened in the premises opposite the building where the prayer group met. Myles felt inspired to pray: "Let the fire of your Spirit fall on these premises". Later that night the premises were destroyed by fire - but no one was hurt. Co-incidence? I do not think so. Soon after that the whole Soho area was largely cleaned up by the police, and I do not doubt that the prayers of the prayer group played a real part in that.

It seems that it is especially evangelical Christians who have been active in this kind of spiritual warfare. For example, they organised days of prayer in the Westminster area of London, where most of the centres of government are situated. About fifty Christians in twos or threes would go and pray before the main centres of power and influence, praising God, rebuking the devil, and asking Jesus to take control of all that happened in the buildings. Similarly, in the London borough of Barnet fasting intercessors went in pairs round the borough, praising God, proclaiming the victory of Jesus, reading the scriptures, rebuking the devil, and interceding. In the above examples the intercession was not done in a way that would attract attention. But there have also been an increasing number of public marches for Jesus in recent years, and these certainly are consciously involved in spiritual warfare.

Catholics would, I think, sometimes find it helpful to be more aware of the spiritual warfare element in their intercessions. For example, Catholic parents whose teenage children have gone or are going off the rails, may find it helpful to know that they are not only praying against human sinfulness and weakness, but that they need also to pray about evil spirits, perhaps of alcoholism, drugs, lust, or the occult. They could pray, normally in their son's absence, "Jesus, please bind any evil spirit of drug addiction troubling our son John, and command it to leave him." However, not everyone would feel at home praying in that sort of way. Pray as the Holy Spirit leads. Going to Mass and offering up their communion for their son or saying the rosary for his intention may be all that is being asked of some people.

I think that parish intercessions could also sometimes be more aware of the spiritual warfare aspect, and there could perhaps be a broadening of the intentions. We are used to praying for the sick, the homeless, and the unemployed in the district - and that is very important. But perhaps we could sometimes pray also, as happens in prayer groups, against the influence of the occult, witchcraft, and Satanism in the district, especially if there had been troublesome signs of these things. For instance, if there is talk of establishing an occult shop in the area - and one such shop not long ago publicly boasted of its courses on Satanism - then surely that is an intention which could be mentioned in the Sunday Masses. And if such a shop is already established, then perhaps the parish could go on the offensive, and pray and work for its removal.

I think that the Christian life becomes more exciting when we take the offensive. Perhaps the words of the old hymn may encourage us:

> Onward, Christian soldiers,
> Marching as to war,
> With the cross of Jesus
> Going on before!
> Christ, the royal Master,
> Leads against the foe;
> Forward into battle
> See, His banners go!

Chapter Seven

The Testimony of a Catholic Psychiatrist

(Dr. F. worked for eight years with the priest exorcist of the diocese)

During my medical studies I had the opportunity in 1974 of meeting with the Charismatic Renewal through a prayer group which had begun a year earlier.

In parallel with my medical studies, I deepened my faith through week-ends of biblical and theological studies, and by training in the discernment of spirits and spiritual counselling.

Once I had become a psychiatrist and was concerned with psychological and spiritual illnesses, I was asked, with the agreement of the bishop to assist a priest-exorcist in his ministry, which was becoming more and more important. The exorcist was on his own in attending to the numerous requests and could rarely speak about it to his brother-priests, who for the most part were afraid of this ministry.

Before telling you of my experience I should like to make certain remarks:

1. It is important that the priest-exorcist should not be alone in exercising this ministry, which must be combined with a great ability to listen and to discern. The help of a psychiatrist is valuable both to elucidate the difficult cases which are part psychological and part spiritual, so that prayer may subsequently be

better directed, and also to be able to assess the ministry of the priest-exorcist, who often finds himself very isolated.

2. It is also important in exercising this ministry to be supported by praying communities and intercessors.

3. If it proves necessary to enlarge the team helping the priest-exorcist, for example if there are many demands on him, for the sake of discretion the team should never be too large. Every member of the team should have a certain experience of listening to people; should be trained in the discernment of spirits; should have a regular and deep-rooted prayer life; be well balanced psychologically and know that Christ has triumphed over all the forces of darkness (Luke 10:17-19; James 4:7; Revelations 12:10-12).

4. What is fundamental for me as a psychiatrist is that every human being is made up of a physical, a psychological, and a spiritual part, as Paul says in the first letter to the Thessalonians (5:23). If one of these parts is not developed the person is unbalanced. Now the good news that Jesus came to bring us is that every person of good will is offered the possibility of liberation and of salvation (and in the etymology of the word salvation there is the word 'health'). Every human being has the possibility, in accepting Jesus as Saviour, of allowing himself or herself to be re-created, to have a change of heart, to have life in abundance, and to find the path to eternal happiness. Who could ever suggest a better future? But this is where the

tempter, the father of lies, can make us believe that by going through him we shall find a better way. This is where our sinful condition makes us succumb to snares, and we find ourselves at a dead end, depressed, discouraged, fettered, imprisoned in our bad habits, with a frantic desire for independence, an inordinate pride, with jealousy, hatred, bitterness, suicidal tendencies, a spirit of lust, or a spirit of idolatry leading us to consult seers, clairvoyants, magicians, workers of spells, etc., which is in contradiction to the word of God in Deuteronomy (18:10-12).

The more we turn away from God and are far from the source of Life, the more our spiritual being is sick and fragile, and this will affect both the psychological and the physical parts of our being. But if we leave ourselves in God's hands, he offers us a way of healing, of purification, of sanctification, in order to become more and more like Him (Genesis 1:26 - "Let us make man in our own image and likeness"). But in order to pass from the image to the likeness we need to let ourselves be moulded during the whole of our life on earth, as Jeremiah says so well in chapter 18:2-6.

My experience as a christian psychiatrist has made me aware of these three dimensions of the human being and not only of the psychological dimension, which by itself is too narrow. Moreover it is important to ask everyone who comes for help about their physical health to detect any cause or causes of his or her present illness or unhappiness. Are the symptoms of physical origin? Are they of psychological origin? Are they of spiritual origin? We need to know this in order to suggest the best treatment to cure the illness. Let us take an example: a forty year old woman has presented a depressive syndrome for several months:

1. On the physical level I shall look at the factors which could be the cause of a depression. If this woman has heavy periods with a beginning of fibroids, she may be losing a lot of blood each month and be deficient in iron. This lack of iron causes tiredness, which will get worse each month, causing anaemia with severe asthenia (debility), which could be the cause of a depressive state. This will be treated with a regular dose of iron, an examination of her fibroids and the support of people coming to assist her in her work, in view of her tiredness - this can be a great help for her. A prayer for healing can also help her, on condition that she continues her medical treatment. Moreover, this iron deficiency, giving rise to a psychological depression, also has spiritual consequences. The depression can bring on a weakening in the spiritual struggle, so that the devil takes advantage of our weakness in order to tempt us. This is true also on the psychological level, where we have less strength to fight against our impulses. Hence the importance in this case of support on the medical, psychological, and spiritual levels.

2. On the psychological level I shall look at the different events which have marked the life of this woman - for example, if she tells me that a few months ago she lost someone dear to her. In this case there is a depressive state consequent upon a bereavement.

It is therefore important to help her by proposing a therapy which will enable her to mourn this person dear to her. Here again, a friendly support in a trusting, caring environment can help this person to come out of her depression. She may even be able, after some time, to help other people who are going through the same trial. If a little group prays for her at her request, this can hasten her cure without short-circuiting the therapy she is having.

3. But her depression may also be of a demonic spiritual origin. For example, she tells me in the course of the consultation that although she is a christian she consulted a clairvoyant about her future. This clairvoyant predicted that she would divorce when she was about forty. This prediction, although she did not entirely believe it, penetrated her mind progressively and subtly, and this woman became anxious. As she was ill at ease with herself, the depression gradually took hold of her even without her thinking again about the clairvoyant's words. I met this particular case quite recently, and in spite of the fact that the interview showed her the link with this clairvoyant, the person concerned was not liberated. That was when I suggested to her a prayer for deliverance. It was the word of authority spoken in the name of Jesus Christ which freed her from this bondage which had deprived her of her liberty. Straight away she felt better and the depression left her. It was then important to look at the causes which had led her to consult a clairvoyant, in order to avoid a recurrence.

This is only one example among many that I have personally encountered. The experience we have in France of the formal prayer of exorcism is fairly limited, because cases of possession are relatively rare. We had a person who had signed a pact with Satan in his blood. This is the only case of possession that I have met of a person who had joined a satanic sect. But prayers for deliverance are much more frequent. Most often these have involved bondages affecting people, for example young people, who 'amused' themselves by making tables turn and who as a result of this experience were disturbed and found themselves unable to work, and for whom a prayer of deliverance was necessary. In effect, when a person gives their trust even unconsciously to an evil spirit, that person is in danger, because the spiritual world is a reality (Ephesians 6:12), even if most psychoanalysts today deny the reality of Satan.

To conclude, I should like to say how much this collaboration with the priest-exorcist has made me grow in faith and trust in God, who has overcome the forces of evil, and has strengthened me in the spiritual combat. I know almost by heart two pages of the Bible that speak of the combat to be waged against the prince of darkness: Ephesians 6 and 1 Peter 5:8-11. This experience has helped me to submit my work to the Lord every day and to pray for the patients who come to see me. I am often surprised to see how much their difficulties or illnesses improve, even if not all get better.

THE TESTIMONY OF A CATHOLIC PSYCHIATRIST

It seems important today that psychiatrists should know about demonic spiritual illnesses which have the appearance of psychological illnesses, because the treatment of these illnesses does not improve, or very little, through medication or psychotherapy. It is through a prayer of deliverance in the name of Jesus, made with discernment and tact, that such illnesses are healed.

Dr. F.

Chapter Eight

Priest-Exorcists' Testimonies

The following testimonies of deliverance and exorcism ministry were all written by Catholic priests who have received the blessing of the bishop for this ministry. All this may be a very new world for some readers, and they may be tempted to disbelieve what they read. May I plead with them to approach this chapter, indeed this whole book, with an open mind. A major problem in the whole field of spiritual warfare is that many Christians seem to be unable or unwilling to face the facts, to recognise what really is happening. Priests appointed by the bishop for this ministry are not likely to be unreliable reporters.

Mary's Life Transformed

Mary (not her real name) was born in 1958 to non-practicing Catholic parents. She was baptised as a baby, and attended a Catholic convent school from 1961 to 1969 where she was prepared for her first communion and confirmation. She liked the religious side of the convent school. In 1969 she was taken elsewhere to live with her father and his girl friend, and Mary lost all contact with the Catholic Church.

Her father's girl friend played with a ouija board, and Mary also became involved with it, acting later sometimes as a medium. This caused disturbances in the home - electrical equipment stopped functioning, and inexplicable heavy footsteps were heard in an upstairs room. Mary also played with the ouija board with some girl friends, which led to what Mary calls a 'bad experience'. One girl went round breaking mirrors, because in the mirrors she was seeing the face of her departed grandfather.

Mary got married in 1976 and later went to live abroad with her husband and three children. In her new country, Mary again had 'bad experiences' in their home, and she discovered that the previous occupants of the house had been spiritualists. Mary had further contact with the occult and she experienced astral and out of the body experiences from time to time. She was told that she was psychically gifted and encouraged to enter further into the occult - she also discovered later that her husband was involved with witchcraft.

On going to live abroad Mary had started practising as a Catholic again; indeed she was active in the Catholic Womens' League and the Society of St. Vincent de Paul - all this alongside her occult involvement!

The marriage broke up. Mary became depressed and twice attempted suicide. She returned to England, and gave up practising as a Catholic because she found a local evangelical charismatic church more uplifting. In 1988 Mary met John (not his real name), a non-practising Catholic, through the social services. John had earlier for some years been a Catholic seminarian. He was now deeply involved in many forms of the occult, esoteric lodges and witchcraft. John performed many occult rituals in

Mary's flat, leading Mary more deeply into the occult, and he gave her a witches gown. On more than one occasion Mary's life was in danger from John.

Mary asked to see me, and I and two women members of our healing team prayed with her on quite a number of occasions, amongst other things casting out any evil spirits of the occult, witchcraft, spiritualism, depression, and suicide. Another priest who was very experienced in this ministry also exorcised Mary.

Accompanied by the two women members of our healing team, I celebrated Mass in Mary's flat, and we cast out any evil spirits which might be there. We also took away and destroyed her tarot cards, cabalistic charts and occult books, which John had left with her. Mary felt that this greatly cleansed the atmosphere in the flat.

After this Mary no longer felt suicidal, was much less depressed, and felt like a different person. She has become a devout Catholic, attending Mass and our Charismatic Prayer Meeting frequently. Mary started studying in the religious studies department at our local university, where she completed her B.A. degree. Her special study, for which she had the Catholic Chaplain as her tutor, was on exorcism. She is now doing a postgraduate degree in a Catholic faculty, and is training as a spiritual director. She hopes later to be employed in pastoral work of some kind. She especially would later like to help free other people from occult involvement.

There is further good news. John, influenced by Mary, has renounced his involvement with the occult, is regularly practicing again as a Catholic, is now training to be a catechist, and will soon complete a course for spiritual directors.

And to think that quite often I was feeling that in our ministry to Mary we were getting nowhere! O, you of little faith!

There is much for which to thank God.

M.H.

God Can Act Quickly

At one of the New Dawn conferences in Walsingham, I was sitting down in the main tent waiting for a talk which was about to begin, when a lady from a European country approached me for ministry. I was not very pleased, since we had just finished a long tiring session of ministry, so I hoped that a short blessing would suffice, but when she began to tell me her story, I reluctantly felt that I had to suggest that we move to a neighbouring tent where there was more privacy and less noise.

The woman had conceived a child in unfortunate circumstances - not her fault - and the child which was born was seriously handicapped. The woman had taken a strong dislike to the child, and her life was largely a spiritual battle to try to love the child as she did her other children. But despite all her efforts, she found herself hating the child, and indeed sometimes hitting the child, to the point that there had been some talk with a social worker about the possible need for the child to be taken into care to protect it from being harmed by the mother.

I felt there was a demonic element in this problem - there seemed to be a force greater than the mother influencing her. So in addition to praying for inner healing, I cast out any evil spirits causing trouble and I cut with the Sword of the Spirit any undue links. The lady said that she felt as if a lump of rock had departed from her stomach when we prayed. The whole ministry took only about ten minutes.

Several months later the same lady came up to me at a Day of Renewal. She had a beautiful smile on her face. She said that since that afternoon in the Walsingham tent she had experienced no problem in loving the handicapped child and that all was now well.

This case prompts in me two reflections. Firstly, the importance of not being in too great a hurry in ministering, even when you are tired. I could easily have made excuses for only spending a couple of minutes with the lady - the talk was about to begin, etcetera ... The second reflection is the thought that there are many people needing and waiting for a brief prayer of deliverance, but there is no one there to say that prayer. How great is the need to develop the deliverance ministry in the Catholic Church!

M.H.

A Pact with Satan

This case concerns a girl, aged between 16 and 17, who had been adopted by excellent Catholic parents. She was one of three adopted children in a family of six; the other three were born to the parents themselves.

The parents made contact with a priest friend because they were concerned by the changes they had observed in the girl's behaviour. She was no longer able to receive Holy Communion, and began leaving the celebration of the Eucharist at the moment the distribution of Communion began. Finally she refused to attend Church altogether. She became a cause of very manipulative disruption in what had been a normally peaceful home.

The priest who interviewed her for the first time discovered that she had previously had some strange experiences: when she looked at the crucifix in the church it seemed to become deformed, and she felt a compulsive desire to destroy the sacred species. It was because of these feelings that she did not want to go to church. Following this, she was filled with fear on meeting a certain priest, whom she had met for the first time on going to a conference with her parents, because when she met him, his face seemed to become deformed as she looked at him.

The priest who first interviewed her then passed her on to me. I asked the parents to take her to a doctor. They did this and he declared her normal: both physically and mentally fit. In spite of this the same problems continued and she was referred back to me.

As a trained counsellor, I started to counsel her and at this point discovered the deeper causes of her present state. She had, approximately nine months before, made a pact with Satan. This involved giving herself over completely to Satan. She had never read anything about such a procedure - only heard it discussed at school because of films other colleagues had seen and talked about.

She found she was able to have 'out of the body experiences' and felt she was disappearing (this never happened in any other person's presence). Moreover, in her own bedroom she carried out a form of devotion to Satan at night.

At this point I discussed the case with another priest - with experience in deliverance. We decided to pray with her. Our decision proved to be the beginning of a process of discernment.

We prayed with her a second time - she had agreed to come only at her parents' request, and also because she was beginning to be paralysed with fear, which was interfering with her living any kind of normal life style. This second experience proved more revealing. We addressed her in several languages during prayer and she replied in all these languages although she could only speak or had studied English. We decided that we needed the Bishop's authority to deal with this, and he gave permission for a formal exorcism, using the old Latin Ritual.

We prepared for this by three days' fasting. We had the help of two religious sisters, since we were dealing with a young woman. We had permission to carry the sacred species on our person, as protection and also to bless the young woman at the appropriate time.

At the very beginning of the exorcism she attacked my fellow priest and removed the pyx from his inside pocket in an instant. Thank God nothing by way of desecration happened. She also, at the beginning, revealed the thoughts in his mind, which at that point were negative towards her.

During the exorcism, which took two attempts, the girl revealed through a very stentorian voice information which afterwards she could not remember. She had lapses of memory - she entered into periods of great confusion and disarray - she levitated, and at times, although slight, could barely be contained by four of us. Her blasphemy, profane language, and lying about people were atrocious. The final straw was when she appeared for the first time to be totally deranged mentally. However, during a time of prayer we discovered she was still under the control of a spirit of falsehood and a spirit of turmoil.

Finally the young woman was released. She became very repentant, has left it all behind her, is now married and has two young children. Last time we met she looked radiant and was attending Church regularly with no further difficulties.

S.C.

An Unusual Case

A local General Practitioner whom I had never met before telephoned me one day. An experience with a person who had visited him in his surgery had suggested something of the paranormal. The doctor, a believer, a good Christian man, suspected an evil presence. The incident that aroused his suspicions was as follows.

The doctor had asked this person to read Ephesians 2 whilst she waited. When she touched the bible it caught fire. The imprint of five finger tips darkened, charred and entered the bible to a depth of approximately twelve pages. I saw that bible, and as always in the case of the very extraordinary, I turned to disbelief - although I am very conscious of the power of Satan. Later that evening, I expressed my disbelief quite openly to the people concerned with the whole incident. However, I started to pray for discernment and guidance. To my amazement, whilst driving to a meeting I turned on the radio in the car and what I heard was the American folk tune - 'The devil came down from Georgia and the flames came out from his fingertips.' How strange the ways God speaks to us!

The following day I agreed to see the person concerned. She refused to talk to me although she had consented to be brought to see me, nor did she look me in the face, and I was unable to help her. A couple of weeks later she rang and asked me to call at her house. It was she herself who reported this time that a neighbour's prayer book caught fire in her hand.

The history behind this story had its basis in frightening unforgiveness. I learned a great lesson through this case of how unforgiveness can open the door to Satanic forces. It is like the house swept clean for the devil's entry and return.

Towards the end of a retreat about a year later this good lady was finally delivered from demonic forces. However, the exorcism was long and involved a lot of patience. She is now very well.

S.C.

The Power of the Mass

Demonic presence in people's homes is an unfortunate reality. We have had to deal with this many times. The following case happened to a very religious young family, husband, wife, and baby. Typical disturbances after they bought the house and went to live in it were: the inexplicable moving of household goods, the hiding of household possessions including keys to doors, the movement and overturning of furniture. Worst of all, household goods moved noiselessly and in an instant from one room to another: for example a washing machine moved suddenly to another room, and bed clothes moved from one room to another. Having blessed a room we moved next door and found the bed linen had moved there before us.

These manifestations required a formal rebuking of the forces of evil. I and another priest were engaged with this case for at least six months. Our investigations involved enquiries about the history of the family who had owned the house previously. There was in that family a history of severed relationships, terrible divisions, particularly between two brothers. While we didn't quite know exactly what was the real source of the dispute, since we were not able to meet the former occupants, nevertheless we had some necessary facts, which included a curse, possibly some occult involvement, also unforgiveness.

The little baby seemed to detect when there were beings around in the house other than humans. Its little eyes followed around and mused on some kind of presence with a variety of body language expressions unusual for a little child. To fully overcome this presence, after many times praying in the house, we celebrated a Mass there. It appears that after the celebration of the Eucharist, and special prayers of protection for the little baby, the hideous and mischievous presence disappeared.

It seems that here was an example where the forces of evil were so entrenched in this house that it took a lot of prayer, patience and endurance to continue in the fight until peace was restored to this young family.

The long history of disturbance was ended and the family resumed their peaceful and happy life.

S.C.

Animals can be Involved

Approximately fifteen years ago I was called to a house with the following two year history of interference. The family had lived in the house for many years before without anything untoward happening. Four children had been born in the family. After a break of ten years a fifth was born. When he reached the age of eight strange things began to happen to him and the house. The child woke at night with something biting him - the actual bites were visible on his whole body, then vomit began to appear on the inner walls of the house. Later, things would fly through the air - including knives and scissors. The situation was so unbearable that the family doctor, having been consulted, accused the 17 year old brother of being responsible. However, that soon became a non-starter when things continued to happen in the absence of the 17 year old from the home. Ministers of other churches, and also a medium, had been called to the house. Ultimately the story reached television and radio.

When I was approached, I was reluctant to be involved because of the publicity. However, I decided to co-operate when the family guaranteed my anonymity. I blessed the home and performed a silent deprecatory exorcism. Three days later the lady of the house reported that things were worse. This time objects were flying all over the place, including when I was in the home. However, although they called my attention to it, I didn't see a green basin floating in the air which was visible to other members of the family.

Again I blessed the house, prayed with the father and mother, and I prayed quietly for a while for discernment. The family had a beautiful St. Bernard dog tied at the foot of the stairs. Into my mind during prayer came the words - "you have prayed with the family but not with the dog". I proceeded to ask questions about the dog. It had been as a puppy the cause of great family division, over who was the original buyer, etcetera. I felt that I should pray over the dog and command the evil to depart. The dog, normally very quiet, went berserk, growled with the most dreadful moans, and after defecating on a beautiful carpet, became quiet again. And so ended the saga, and peace returned to the family and home. The dog had been the instrument of dissension and appeared to carry some kind of evil presence into an otherwise lovely family. One remembers the case in the gospel of the evil spirits who entered the pigs.

The long history of disturbance was ended and the

family resumed their peaceful and happy life. However, obviously evil spirits entering animals is relatively rare.

S.C.

A Case of Witchcraft

I had been invited to a high level conference of academics, dealing with the study of magic and witchcraft phenomena. Specialists had come from different European countries. Personally, I was to speak about magic phenomena in our day.

As I came out after giving my talk, a member of the audience approached me and said: "What you have been talking about corresponds exactly with what I am going through. I am a priest, and this is what happened to me:

"I was in a mission in a large African town. I had built several houses to make a children's village, with a team of black workers from that country. Then I received the gift of a considerable sum of money from an international organisation. With this money I engaged a second team of workers from another tribe. When the work was finished, the second team said to me: "Father, don't sleep in these houses, you will see, you will be ill, look ..." They lifted some tiles from the floor and showed me some 'fetish' objects. They unstuck some paper and showed me other bizarre objects. "Father, these are objects consecrated to the devil. They are furious against us because we are from another tribe and you have employed us. They have taken revenge and they want to kill you."

As a good European rationalist I didn't take any notice, smiling patronisingly to myself.

The following night I slept in that house, or rather I didn't sleep at all. I was tormented by all sorts of images and mad ideas and was so ill at ease in my body that I found it impossible to sleep. After a few sleepless nights I became tortured by the wish to commit suicide.

I was taken to hospital, where they succeeded in preventing me from committing suicide. On the other hand, all the analyses were in order and the psychological tests revealed nothing.

I had to be repatriated. For years in France I went from one clinic to another without result. I was accepted into a home for sick priests, where they couldn't find anything. Now I am in a home for aged and infirm priests and I recognise myself in the signs that you have indicated."

I was very tired, as I had just had an operation. I had to lie on a bed to make a long prayer of deliverance. He was very shaken and prayed with me with all his soul. I wasn't able to release him that evening. The next day we began again at length, and finally he was released.

He was able to leave the home for aged and infirm priests and, having recovered the strength of his youth, he left again for a far-off mission. He has been working there for four years. His deliverance was definitive and he had no need of further intervention.

An Old People's Home

It happened in an old people's home in Yorkshire. There was a matron, and a staff of younger people. I remember there were three men among them who were not given to imagination or to praying. But there was an atmosphere of jumpiness among them after the phenomena which I am about to relate. They cared for perhaps a hundred residents.

We set up a meeting to hear about the situation. There was the local Catholic priest, and myself - the recognised priest in the diocese for this kind of ministry. Also present were a lady Methodist minister and a retired Anglican priest.

We heard these facts: first, there was an old-time nanny and two children from a century ago, who were so frequently seen about the place that the residents thought they were part of the establishment. The children used to come sometimes to their rooms and visit. Less frequently there appeared a monk and a nun from some previous age.

These restless visitors were not idle or harmless. Their favourite trick was to tamper with the fire-fighting equipment, causing anxiety and expense. There were times when the extinguishers were visibly interfered with by some unseen hand. Very often they were found dry, even after having been serviced.

In one of the rooms the unfortunate person to whom it was allotted, though well up to that point, became ill and died unexpectedly. This happened on three occasions in that room. When an attendant touched the wall in one of the rooms he felt a strong vibration and had great difficulty in getting his hand away.

Another young man was terrified when as he

walked home he felt that he was being followed by a menacing ghostly presence on many occasions.

So we arranged for a time we could go into the home when all the residents would be having their tea in the dining room. We first spoke to the staff, all of whom were aware of something quite unusual and disturbing, but not all aware of the power of Jesus Christ. We did not want to be mistaken for some kind of witch-doctors! We then set out and went through the building praying for the faithful departed, and claiming each room for Christ, by anointing with blest oil, and using holy water. Perhaps this took about an hour. We arranged for Mass to be offered, though not on the premises.

Some time later the local Parish Priest informed me that the disturbances had totally ceased.

We learned two historical facts, though there was some uncertainly about the first: that there had been a monastery and/or convent on the site in medieval times. The second was that a family home built later on the site had been destroyed by fire.

M.K.

Chapter Nine

The Challenge

The Christian religion is centred on Jesus, not on the devil. Our concentration should be very much on Jesus. Too much thinking and talking about the devil and demons gives them an honour which is not due to them. That is 'demonitis'. However, to ignore totally the existence of the devil and demons is not right either, and that is a much more common failing among Catholics today, at any rate in many countries.

When did you last hear the devil mentioned in a parish sermon? I would think that in some parishes the devil has not been mentioned in a sermon for many years. God forbid that we should have frequent sermons on the devil! But it is not right either simply to forget his existence. As has often been said, one of the greatest triumphs of the devil in our times has been to make many Christians think that he does not exist, or at any rate to act as if he did not exist. He can work more powerfully when we ignore his existence.

Why do a number of priests never mention the devil in a sermon? Because some priests do not think that he exists, other priests are uncertain as to whether or not he exists, other priests would not want to frighten people - but if there is a real danger of fire, we should not refrain from mentioning it in order not to frighten people! Still other priests would simply not know what to say about the devil, even when they do in fact believe that he exists.

It is not only a matter of sermons. There is also the question of individual counselling and ministry. Many priests would never suggest to a person in distress that they were perhaps being troubled or attacked by the devil. Nor would some priests say that it was important not to play with ouija boards and tarot cards, because it can open people up to demonic troubles.

I do not however wish to judge and blame individual priests. What preparation did they receive in this area in the seminary? I personally have spoken to two priests who lectured in seminaries and who could not affirm that they believed in the existence of a personal devil - one said that perhaps in five years time he may do so. So having received little or no instruction in these matters in the seminary, the priest is understandably at a loss what to preach or advise in this area.

Father Jim McManus CSSR, now provincial of the Redemptorists in this country, writes in his remarkable book, 'Healing in the Spirit. Ministry of Healing in Today's Church' (DLT): "I had taught moral and pastoral theology to students for the priesthood for six years and I had never even mentioned a ministry of deliverance or exorcism. Looking back on those years I have to say that although I never formally gave up belief in the Church's teaching on evil spirits, my faith was totally inactive. I was aware that possession by the devil could take place in rare cases. I was also aware that if that happened the bishop would appoint a holy, wise, and ascetical priest to deal with it. It would be no concern of mine. I realised that throughout the Catholic Church, in most, if not in all the seminaries where priests were being trained, there would be no teaching on this ministry. That is why I said that I understand why so many priests and ministers don't use this ministry. Like myself, nobody taught them about it." (page 111). Father Jim has since those days developed a powerful ministry of inner healing and deliverance, as readers of his book will discover.

Because quite a number of needy Catholics are not receiving any or much instruction or help in their own church in the field of deliverance or protection from evil spirits, quite a few of them are going to other Christians for this help. I know several Anglican priests experienced in the deliverance ministry who have over the years been receiving quite a stream of Catholics for this ministry. And other Catholics have been going to Pentecostals and other Evangelicals. Cross fertilisation in the healing ministry can be a good thing in the ecumenical age in which we live, but there can sometimes be a danger of Catholics being over influenced by teaching which is not in line with the Catholic way of seeing things, for example being told that all alternative therapy is demonic, or that all inter-faith dialogue is of the devil, or that it is wrong to ask Our Lady to pray for you.

Every Pentecostal minister would not only firmly believe in the existence of the devil and evil spirits, he would also have received some training in recognising when people need deliverance from evil spirits and in how to exercise this ministry. So it is understandable that some Catholics in need of deliverance may go to a Pentecostal pastor, rather than a Catholic priest who may not believe in the existence of the devil.

There are also the problems posed by the difficulty for Catholics who need serious exorcism ministry of finding an approved Catholic exorcist. Despite canon law, in some dioceses no provision is made for this ministry. And where a priest is appointed for this ministry, it may in practice be very difficult for the needy person to get to him, and if he does get to him he may find that the 'exorcist' more or less limits his ministry to sending people to psychiatrists - which was the stated policy of one diocese in the USA of which I heard.

Some years ago a Catholic man in a prayer group in the USA felt the need for exorcism ministry. His request was passed on to the diocesan chancery, who spent six months making enquiries and considering the question. The man lost patience, and one evening he walked down the road to the local Pentecostal church, where he was effectively delivered from evil spirits in half an hour.

There can be other practical problems. A very experienced Anglican priest exorcist told me of a sad case. He was asked if he would minister to a person in another diocese. The local Anglican bishop was consulted and insisted that a psychiatrist be consulted first. Arrangements were being made for the person to see a psychiatrist but before this could happen, the depressed person committed suicide. The general principle of consultation between exorcists and the medical profession is an excellent one but when people are feeling suicidal or violent, delay in receiving exorcism ministry may be fatal, as it was with the man mentioned above.

In case people think I am exaggerating, I will refer to the book by the official exorcist of the diocese of Rome: 'Un esorcisto racconta', by Gabriele Amorth, (Edizioni Dehoniane, Rome 1990). In the Introduction he relates how on being appointed official exorcist for the diocese of Rome he discovered that there were very few official exorcists in Italy and that these had received very little training. He goes on to say that the situation is worse in some other countries, and complains that he has had to minister to people from France, Austria, Germany, Switzerland, and England, because needy people had not been able to find this ministry in their own country. He asks whether this is because priests and bishops do not believe in the need for, and fruitfulness of, this ministry. He goes on to say that in the Catholic world pastoral practice in this field is totally neglected ("e deltutto trascurata"). It was not always so in the past, he continues, and we must recognise that it is not so in certain protestant denominations, in which exorcisms are taking place often and fruitfully. He suggests that every cathedral should have an exorcist, as also major parishes and sanctuaries.

Gabriele Amorth is his book describes a telephone call he received from a bishop elsewhere in Italy. The bishop asked him if he could see someone for exorcism from his diocese. Amorth suggested that instead the bishop should appoint a priest in his diocese for this ministry. The bishop said there was no one he could appoint. Amorth then suggested that the bishop should exorcise the person himself, to which the bishop replied that he would not know where to begin. That is an important point. It is not enough to appoint a priest as official exorcist. There needs to be some training. It is to the credit of the diocese in which I live that the bishop sent a priest to Rome to be trained in this ministry.

Now for another important point. It has been our experience in the healing ministry of the Catholic Charismatic Renewal that not only priests but also some religious sisters and some lay people have received special gifts of healing in the deliverance-exorcism area. (I use the word 'exorcism' to describe the heavier and more serious end of the deliverance ministry.) I myself have in this field ministered with the help of lay people who were clearly more gifted than myself. What use is the Catholic Church making of these gifted people? Does God want gifted lay Pentecostals to be able to exercise this ministry but not gifted lay Catholics? In his book, 'Renewal and the Power of Darkness' (DLT 1983), Cardinal Suenens makes an interesting suggestion: "I would add that if the office of exorcist has disappeared as a minor order, there is nothing to prevent an episcopal conference from requesting Rome to restore it. I do not know if this is advisable, but it is at least a possibility which is deserving of study. If the conclusion is positive, then the office of exorcist could be made available to qualified laymen." (page 97)

As the Irish bishops said in their recent very positive statement about the Charismatic Renewal (1993): "In the Charismatic Renewal there is an awareness of the operation of the power of Satan" - an awareness which seems to be missing in so much of the life of the rest of the Catholic Church. I think that in practice much of the effective deliverance-exorcism ministry in the Catholic Church today is being done by Catholics involved in the Charismatic Renewal. I think that more and more bishops are using priests involved in the Charismatic Renewal for this ministry, to judge from priests with whom I have talked on this subject.

So it is difficult to avoid the conclusion that in the whole field of deliverance-exorcism ministry, the Pentecostals and the evangelical Charismatics are in general much more active and indeed more competent than Catholics. I would think that in general a non-believer who found himself badly caught up in demonic troubles because of involvement with the occult would be more likely to receive the help he needed from the Pentecostal-Evangelical side than from a Catholic priest. I remember one such case, and the man himself after being delivered joined an evangelical church and developed a powerful healing ministry. The Catholic priest whom he had approached simply could not help him.

On the Catholic side we are hampered by unbelief in the existence of demons, by ignorance about the deliverance ministry, and by very tight regulations. Surely we need to wake up, we need a real renewal of the deliverance-exorcism ministry in the Catholic Church, as the official exorcist for the diocese of Rome pleads with all his heart and mind in his book.

There is, however, another side to this whole

question, and we must mention that now. Things can go very wrong in the exorcism ministry and sometimes do. For example, a few years ago in the London borough in which I live, a wandering evangelical preacher and his friend attempted to exorcise a woman at her request. In trying to get the demons out of her they stamped on her body - and this killed her. They then prayed for twelve hours for her return to life, which needless to say did not happen. They then handed themselves over to the police. Then there was the famous Barnsley case in 1974, when after an all-night exorcism session a man went home and killed his wife in a most brutal manner. So the Catholic Church is quite rightly cautious, and she rightly does not believe in allowing anyone and everyone to undertake the ministry of exorcism.

Although many Pentecostal and Evangelical Churches have a serious discipline when it comes to the ministry of exorcism and are very careful as to whom they allow to minister in this field, there are nevertheless sometimes excesses on the evangelical side. Needless to say, as a Catholic I was not happy about the well-known evangelical exorcist who used to cast out 'evil spirits of Romanism' from Catholics who came to him for ministry!

Nor am I happy about the following passage from the book by the leader of a well-known evangelical healing centre: "After conversion the man renounced all his New Age beliefs, but remained a vegetarian because he thought it made sense.

"Whilst ministering to him the Lord drew my attention to this by Word of Knowledge, and I asked him therefore, if he would renounce vegetarianism also. He declined, the demons would not go and I was unable to minister to him any further. An hour later he was back, realising that if the demons that had come into him through his New Age involvements would not go, because his vegetarianism was giving them a legal right to be there, he would prefer to give up being a vegetarian than continue to be demonised!

"Immediately he renounced vegetarianism he was free to be delivered and in a relatively short period of time a large number of spirits left. Refusing to eat all that God had made available for him to eat had given sufficient ground to the enemy for him to be held deeply in bondage, graphically demonstrating the truth of Paul's words to Timothy about the teachings of demons!" Are we to believe that the many generations of monks who abstained from eating meat were all demonised by evil spirits of vegetarianism?

Exaggerations of this kind bring the ministry of deliverance into disrepute. If we are seeing demons where there are no demons, then people will not listen to us when we warn them about the danger of demons which really do exist.

Obviously the Catholic Church needs to keep a balance between caution and confidence when it comes to the exorcism ministry. One can be over-cautious or over-confident. If we are over-cautious, then we shall fail to help needy people - often very desperately needy people - whom we should be helping. If we are over-confident, then there will be casualties. It seems to me that at present we are in general clearly erring very much on the side of over-caution, so that we are failing in our duty to help people. One priest who has exercised this ministry with the blessing of his bishop once said to me that fear of the tabloid press was too often the dominant factor. If we are taking the line that whatever else happens we must never under any circumstance risk the possibility of an exorcism scandal in the popular press, then we shall be paralysed by fear and prevented from helping people. Perhaps there is a parallel with medical surgery. We all read in the press from time to time about cases in which surgery has gone very wrong. The only way to make absolutely certain that nothing could ever go wrong in surgery would be to perform no operations. Some people would take this line with exorcism, and thus nullify the Lord's promise that "by using my name they will cast out demons" (Mark 16:17).

It is however clearly important to cut down as far as reasonably possible the risk of things going wrong in the exorcism ministry, and some things can help us here. The first point is to do as much healing and liberating as we can through the ministry of inner healing. There can be a considerable over-lapping between praying for inner healing and deliverance ministry - deliverance ministry should normally be accompanied by payer for inner healing and for the infilling of the Holy Spirit. Sometimes - but not always - prayer for inner healing will suffice to deliver someone from evil spirits.

The second point is that concentrating on the healing power of the sacraments can sometimes - but not always - suffice to liberate people from evil spirits.

We should not under-estimate the healing and liberating power of the sacraments. However, there remains a place for casting out evil spirits. In the New Testament Church the sacraments were not a substitute for the casting out of evil spirits.

A final point worth making here is that there is nothing to be gained from trying to cast evil spirits out of someone who is not willing to repent of and renounce the sins or practices which allowed evil spirits to enter. So if someone is having trouble with evil spirits because of involvement with the occult, then they need to repent of and renounce that involvement before we try to liberate them. As long as someone holds on to the occult involvement, the evil spirits have in a sense the right to be there. I have met people who wanted to be liberated from the unpleasant effects of evil spirits but were not willing to try to give up the practices which had let the evil spirits in. Trying to cast evil spirits out of people who are not willing to repent and renounce can lead to trouble, and in any case is a waste of time and energy. In such cases we need to pray that they will be given the grace to repent and renounce.

Chapter Ten

Further Challenges

Another urgent area of challenge is that of warning Catholics - and anyone else who will listen to us - of the dangers of involvement in the occult. Children in schools, including Catholic schools, are playing with ouija boards and tarot cards. In Catholic schools there are sometimes Halloween parties of a kind which have no place in a Christian institution. In Catholic parishes there are sometimes fortune-telling stalls in parish bazaars. In case someone thinks I am exaggerating, I will give some examples:

At one Catholic cathedral a day of celebration was announced, with a special Mass to be celebrated by a bishop. On the notice announcing all this, a list of events was advertised, and one was a palm- reading stall. (This stall was in fact dropped as a result of protests.) I can think of several cases of parish bazaars with fortune-telling stalls - and serious ones. One was dropped as a result of protests. In another case the parish priest told a woman who objected that if she did not like the stall she could transfer to another parish. In a Catholic school there was a Mass celebrated at Halloween, and the walls of the room where the Mass was celebrated were decorated for the occasion with lots of sweet-looking witches flying around on broomsticks. (One member of the staff refused to attend the Mass as a protest.) This reminds me of the Catholic mother in a house I was recently asked to bless who had placed a cloth witch hanging from the ceiling by the bed of her daughter "as a protection for my daughter". Finally, a priest who is the official exorcist for his diocese told me that he had heard of a "great many cases of children playing with ouija boards in schools".

Now that the new Catechism has appeared, which is very definite about the existence of the devil and demons and equally clear that involvement in the occult and fortune-telling are definitely out for a Catholic, we can surely hope that the bishops, the clergy, and catechists will remind Catholics of the teaching of the Bible and the Church in these areas. And the Catholic Church can warn the wider public of the dangers of demonic trouble arising from involvement in the occult.

Another area of challenge is that of the personal lives of individuals. Christians need to be aware that we are all being attacked at times by the devil, that we are all involved in spiritual warfare. The love of God and our neighbour is the key to holiness, not belief in a personal devil. And some Christians who do not believe in a personal devil are more holy than some Christians who do. Nevertheless, an awareness of the existence of personal demonic forces is normally an aid to growth in holiness, for it helps us to understand better the nature of the spiritual life. So there is a need for Catholics to be reminded of this area of Catholic tradition, but avoiding exaggerations. The clergy surely have here a special responsibility in their roles as teachers and spiritual guides. Furthermore, I think that not only reading the Bible can be important here, but also reading the spiritual classics. The saints and major spiritual writers are aware that we are involved in spiritual warfare with demonic forces. In a way, the point made in this paragraph may be more important than some of the more dramatic things mentioned earlier in this book. To get the ordinary Catholic prepared for his or her spiritual warfare is doubtless more necessary than dealing with the far fewer people who need exorcism ministry, important though the latter is.

It has become obvious to all thinking people that we are living in very extraordinary times. Humankind now has developed the power to destroy human life on earth. When we remember what harm a relatively small accident like Chernobyl did, it is not difficult to imagine what harm could be done by mad leaders in an all-out war - and history has thrown up mad leaders from time to time: one has only to think of Hitler. Then there is the whole environmental and ecological crisis, with the increasing pollution of our planet. And there are new illnesses like Aids, and also the increasing problem of drug abuse.

In the face of all this, and reflecting on the significance of the return of the Jews to Israel, increasing numbers of Christians are convinced that the Second Coming of Jesus is imminent. This conviction is held by all Pentecostal Christians, many other Evangelicals, and I have met Catholics who also think on those lines. I personally do not share that definite conviction, but I must say that I do not regard it as being in any way a lunatic fringe opinion, and they may be right. In any case, all Christians should in a sense be looking forward to the return of the Lord. All Christians can say with the book of Revelation: "Maranatha. Come, Lord Jesus!" (Rev. 22:20) even if it is not for their life time.

(I hope that I will excused if I point out to the Pentecostals that for nearly a hundred years now they have been saying that the return of the Lord was imminent. Perhaps we are at the beginning of a very new period of human history on earth rather than at the end of it - this is the view to which I incline.)

However, I am not claiming to be a prophet when it comes to predicting the future of humankind - I do not think that I am called to that role. But I do wish to say as strongly as I can that in the tensions, clashes, and dangers of our times the devil is especially active. He is a defeated foe, the final outcome of the battle is certain, the final victory of Jesus is being worked out. However, in the meantime Satan is causing a lot of trouble, and may well cause even greater trouble in the coming years.

The words of Vatican II in the Dogmatic Constitution on the Church (paragraph 16) apply, I think, in a very special way to the times in which we live: "For a monumental struggle against the powers of darkness pervades the whole history of man. The battle was joined from the very origins of the whole world and will continue until the last day, as the Lord attested (cf. Matthew 24:13; 13:24-30, 36-43). Caught in this conflict man is obliged to wrestle constantly if he is to cling to what is good. Nor can he achieve his own integrity without valiant efforts and the help of God's grace". The above words are true for every age, but it is only in our times that human-kind has developed powers which could possibly bring human life on earth to an end. In that sense the situation is different now, the dangers are now far greater. As Christians we know that Jesus is Lord of this situation, that he will limit the evil that Satan is allowed to do. As Christians we can be hopeful, because we put our trust in Jesus.

Now I come to an ecumenically delicate subject, but one which, I think, honesty demands that I do not try to avoid: the role of Mary, the mother of Jesus, especially in our times. A considerable number of Catholics - and not a few other Christians - are convinced that in our times Jesus is in a special way making use of his mother in bringing people to Himself, and in combating the activity of Satan. Of course, "there is only one mediator between God and human-kind, Christ Jesus, himself human, who gave himself a ransom for all" (Timothy 2:5). Jesus is our only Saviour. But Catholics and many other Christians believe that Jesus listens to the prayers of his mother.

I am thinking largely of the apparitions of Our Lady in Medjugorje and elsewhere, which seem to be increasing in number in recent years. What are we to think of these apparitions? I remember one good priest, now dead, who had a very real devotion to Our Lady, who once said to me that he was not interested in apparitions of Our Lady. It is not necessary to be interested in Medjugorje and similar places in order to love Our Lady, and to ask for her prayers. However, I think that if we honestly face up to the facts we shall have to admit that very many people who go to Medjugorje and similar places are coming to a new or greater knowledge and love of Jesus as a result of going there. I have met a considerable number of people who have been converted or more deeply converted to Jesus at Medjugorje. Indeed, I think my own two visits to Medjugorje and my reading of literature connected with it have increased my knowledge and love of Jesus. So I would particularly ask our evangelical friends, many of whom are such wonderful Christians, to judge the apparitions of Medjugorje and similar places by the test of what influence they are having on people's relationship with Jesus.

Some Catholics will wish to limit their interest in shrines of Our Lady to places where the apparitions have been officially approved, such as Lourdes in France (1858), Fatima in Portugal (1917), and Banneaux in Belgium (1933). Fair enough. No one is obliged to go, for example, to Medjugorje. However, it is worth mentioning that a certain number of the recent apparitions have already been officially approved, for example: Akita in Japan (1973), Kibeho in Rwanda (1981), and Betania in Venezuela (1981).

Others appear to be on the way towards official approval, for example, San Nicholas in Argentina (1983), where the local bishop is very supportive. Moreover, there are the recent apparitions which have been officially approved by the Eastern Churches, such as those in Cairo, where Our Lady was seen by many thousands of people.

However, though I believe that Our Lady really is powerfully active in Medjugorje and in an apparently increasing number of similar places, I am also convinced that there are a number of false apparitions, in which the devil plays his part. Moreover, I do not think it is just a question of black or white - there can be various degrees of grey.

I must also add that I am not entirely happy with some literature connected with apparitions of Our Lady in which the name of Mary is mentioned so much more often than the name of Jesus. Nor am I entirely happy with religious art which seems to place Jesus and Mary on the same level. Mary is always wanting to lead us to Jesus, is always wanting the main thrust to be very much on Jesus. So I think that she herself is not happy when we appear to be putting her on the same level as her son. Some Catholic literature and religious art would almost seem to be deliberately making it more difficult for evangelicals to understand the true Catholic teaching on Mary, the mother of Jesus!

Now we come to the final challenge in these chapters,

the challenge of Christian unity. Jesus prayed "that they may all be one. As you, Father, are in me and I am in you, may they also be one in us, so that the world may believe that you have sent me" (John 17:21). Perhaps the devil's greatest success over the centuries has been to divide the disciples of Jesus and to create hostility between them. I am particularly thinking in this chapter of the disunity, ignorance, prejudice, and often hostility which frequently exists in the relationships between Evangelicals and Pentecostals on the one side and Catholics on the other.

I write as someone who is a convinced Catholic, but I recognise that the Holy Spirit is working powerfully among Evangelicals and Pentecostals. Moreover, on the subject of this book, spiritual warfare, I think we Catholics can often learn from the example of the Evangelicals and Pentecostals. So frequently we Catholics seem to be silent, while it is left to the Evangelicals and Pentecostals to point out the dangers of the occult, witchcraft, satanism, and things connected with them. One is not surprised that it was, for example, an Evangelical, David Porter, who wrote the excellent book, 'Halloween Treat or Trick' (Monarch), pointing out the dangers of many Halloween celebrations. It seems to be left largely to Evangelicals and Pentecostals to warn us about games like Dungeons and Dragons, and some children's toys, and other harmful influences on children.

Yes, Evangelicals and Pentecostals do sometimes exaggerate - and I have felt bound to point out in this book some of these exaggerations, as I see things. But I think our debt to the Evangelicals and Pentecostals far more than outweighs the harm done by their exaggerations.

I pray that Catholics will wake up in the whole area of spiritual warfare, and that we shall work together with Evangelicals and Pentecostals - and with anyone willing to work with us - in our common battle against the devil, serving together our common saviour, Jesus, and drawing closer to each other as we do so.

Come Holy Spirit !

Epilogue

The writing of this book has been a very difficult task. No sooner had I started collecting material than I was hit by illness, which postponed work on the book. Then there were considerable and unexpected delays over publishers, until I got in touch with New Life Publishing, who could not have been more helpful, encouraging, and rapid. Certainly I have had the impression that the devil was anxious to prevent the book being published.

However, I have also had the impression that the need for a book of this kind is increasingly urgent. Many Catholics, and also other Christians, need to wake up to the reality of the spiritual warfare in which we are all involved individually and collectively. For instance, I have before me a public advertisement for 'The Little Voodoo Kit Revenge Therapy', which includes 'a small voodoo doll and six pins'. (Sticking pins into dolls has long been a traditional witchcraft way of cursing people.) A Japanese advertisement for a similar product is more open, and calls it a 'cursing kit'. Surely the time has come for Christians and other people of good will to work for the legal banning of the selling and advertising of things of this kind.

Then there is the whole question of satanism. Not so infrequently, horrific crimes are in one way or another linked with satanism. For example, Harrett Campbell, who was recently "found guilty on seven counts of attempted murder", ran amok among young children in a nursery school with a machete blade on which he had written "666 Marks the Devil". He also "wore a deer stalker hat with two bolts attached on each side resembling the horns of a devil". (The Times 10.12.96, page 1)

Then there is the recent news from Belgium; "Satanic sects involved in bizarre rites including human sacrifice are being linked by Belgian police with this summer's string of grisly paedophile murders in which at least four children died. Five witnesses came forward last week and described how black masses were held, at which children were killed in front of audiences said to have included prominent members of Belgian society..... The witnesses - several of whom claim to have received death threats - say that young babies were handed over by their parents willingly in return for money. In other cases the victims were abducted." (The Sunday Times, 29.12.96, page 14).

Being convinced of the truthfulness of very similar accounts given me by a woman I was recently trying to help, I have no difficulty in believing the above reports from Belgium.

A priest friend of mine who was for a time a chaplain to a small prison in the USA reckoned that about 10% of the prisoners were satanists. Indeed, the satanists in the prison had asked the prison governor to allow them to meet regularly for the worship of Satan, since satanism is an officially recognised religion in the USA. The governor had refused permission. If there is that sort of link between crime and satanism in the USA, are we to suppose that there is not also a real link in this country and elsewhere? If this is so, should not Christians and other people of good will be working for the banning of satanism by law - something which surely could be done without endangering true freedom of religion?

In our Catholic parishes we very rightly often pray in the bidding prayers of Mass for such intentions as peace in the world, the unemployed, and the homeless. Should we not also be praying sometimes against the dangers of witchcraft, satanism, and the spread of paganism? Bishops and other Church leaders rightly speak out strongly on questions of social justice. Should they not also be speaking out about the dangers of the occult? Is it right that the latter concern should be left largely to evangelical and Pentecostal Christians?

However, I do not wish to be pessimistic about the situation in the Catholic Church. An increasing number of official priest exorcists are being appointed, at any rate in some countries. There are now regular gatherings for priest exorcists in certain countries, and also at the international level, and the number of priests coming to some of these gatherings is increasing rapidly. Francis MacNutt has written a book on the deliverance ministry 'Deliverance from Evil Spirits, a Practical Manual', Chosen Books, Baker Book House, USA (1995) and published in England by Hodder and Stoughton. I think this will become a classic, as his previous book Healing (1974) has been for the healing ministry.

My smaller book, however, is intended for a much wider public. It is an introduction to the subject of spiritual warfare for the ordinary priest and lay person. It seeks to help the ordinary Christian in his or her ongoing battle with the forces of darkness, warning them of dangers, and giving them helpful advice and confidence in the victory of Jesus over a defeated foe. It might be a suitable book to lend or give to your parish priest, especially if he is not certain whether the devil exists.

Some of the people who read this book may think that perhaps they themselves, or a member of their family, or one of their friends, or their house may be in need of some form of explicit deliverance ministry. Perhaps they themselves are troubled by inexplicable experiences or harmful compulsions, over which the doctors cannot help, perhaps one of their children is behaving in strange ways which the doctors cannot understand, perhaps strange noises or happenings are being experienced in their home. What can they do about it?

Catholics should normally start by consulting their parish priest. He might deal with the problem himself, or he might suggest that they should see the diocesan exorcist - if there is one - or they themselves could ask to see the diocesan exorcist. It is of course always possible for Catholics to approach their bishop directly.

If you are a Catholic and have decided to look for help elsewhere, please be very careful where you go. Some Catholic priests and lay people, especially in the Charismatic Renewal, do have gifted and reliable healing and deliverance ministries, as do some clergy and lay people in other Christian churches - for example, the Anglican Church has a network of official exorcists in this country. However, it is very important not to go to Spiritualists, or to people involved in the occult, because this could lead to disasters. Only recently I saw a Catholic lay minister of communion who has been very badly damaged by someone who was trying to heal her through Tibetan magic.

At the end of the main body of this book, may I suggest that the reader should pause for prayer, both for themselves and for other readers, not a few of whom may be going through difficult struggles in their spiritual warfare. May the Holy Spirit guide, strengthen, protect, heal, and anoint us all.

Herons have long necks, and in this book I have stuck out my own neck not a little. So perhaps some readers may like to spare a prayer for the author and also the publishers of this book. Thank you.

Appendix One

Some Official Texts of the Catholic Church on Angels and Demons

In this appendix we shall see a selection of official texts of the Catholic Church concerning angels and demons. These texts will include some from the official liturgy of the Church, which has always been seen as a source of belief.

The Second Vatican Council in its Dogmatic Constitution on the Church refers to: "When the Lord will come in glory, and all his angels with him" (cf Matthew 25:31) (49). And in the next paragraph (50), referring to the apostles and martyrs, the Constitution says that the Church "has always enrolled them, together with the Blessed Virgin Mary and the holy angels, with a special love, and has asked piously for the help of their intercession".

In Vatican II's Constitution on the Sacred Liturgy (Chapter 1:6), we read that the "Son of God, by his death and resurrection, had freed us from the power of Satan (cf Acts 26:18) and from death, and brought us into the Kingdom of his Father". In the Decree on the Church's Missionary Activity there are two references to the devil. The Father sent Jesus into the world that "he might snatch men from the power of darkness and of Satan (cf Colossians 1:13, Acts 10:38) and in him reconcile the world to himself" (3). And in paragraph 9 we read of Christ "who overthrows the rule of the devil and limits the manifold malice of evil".

In the Dogmatic Constitution on the Church there are also references to the demonic. In paragraph 16 we read: "But very often, deceived by the Evil One, men have become vain in their reasonings, have exchanged the truth of God for a lie and served the world rather than the Creator." Finally, in paragraph 37 there is a passage which is very important for the theme of this book: "For a monumental struggle against the powers of darkness pervades the whole history of man. The battle was joined from the very origins of the whole world and will continue until the last day, as the Lord has attested (cf Matthew13:24-30 and 36-43, 24:13). Caught in this conflict man is obliged to wrestle constantly if he is to cling to what is good. Nor can he achieve his own integrity without valiant efforts and the help of God's grace".

In the new universal Catechism of the Catholic Church there are a considerable number of references to angels and demons. Here we will limit ourselves to two major texts which give a wide general view of the Catholic Church's teaching on angels and demons. It is worth quoting these texts in full, so that the reader can see clearly what is the official mind of the Catholic Church on this subject. It is to be hoped that the appearance of the new universal Catechism will help to affirm the faith of some Catholics whose minds had begun to wobble on the subject of angels and demons - as, indeed, doubtless on other truths of the Christian faith also.

1. The Angels

The Existence of Angels - a Truth of Faith

328: The existence of the spiritual, non-corporeal beings that Sacred Scripture usually calls 'angels' is a truth of faith. The witness of Scripture is as clear as the unanimity of Tradition.

Who are They?

329: St. Augustine says: " 'Angel' is the name of their office, not of their nature. If you seek the name of their nature, it is 'spirit'; if you seek the name of their office, it is 'angel': from what they are, 'spirit', from what they do 'angel'."[188] With their whole beings the angels are servants and messengers of God. Because they "always behold the face of my Father who is in heaven" they are the "mighty ones who do his word, hearkening to the voice of his word".[189]

330: As purely spiritual creatures angels have intelligence and will: they are personal and immortal creatures, surpassing in perfection all visible creatures, as the splendour of their glory bears witness.[190]

Christ "With all his Angels"

331: Christ is the centre of the angelic world. They are his angels: "When the Son of Man comes in his glory, and all the angels with him..."[191] They belong to him because they were created through and for him: "For in him all things were created in heaven and on earth, visible and invisible, whether thrones or dominions, or principalities or authorities - all things were created through him and for him."[192] They belong to him still more because he has made them messengers of his saving plan: "Are they not all ministering spirits sent forth to serve, for the sake of those who are to obtain salvation?"[193]

332: Angels have been present since creation and throughout the history of salvation, announcing this salvation from afar or near and serving the accomplishment of the divine plan: they closed the earthly paradise; protected Lot; saved Hagar and her child; stayed Abraham's hand; communicated the law by their ministry; led the People of God; announced births and callings; and assisted the prophets, just to cite a few examples.[194] Finally, the angel Gabriel announced the birth of the Precursor and that of Jesus himself.[195]

333: From the Incarnation to the Ascension, the life of the Word incarnate is surrounded by the adoration and service of angels. When God 'brings the firstborn into the world, he says: "Let all God's angels worship him".'[196] Their song of praise at the birth of Christ has not ceased resounding in the Church's praise: "Glory to God in the highest!"[197] They protect Jesus in his infancy; serve him in the desert; strengthen him in his agony in the garden, when he could have been saved by them from the hands of his enemies as Israel had been.[198] Again, it is the angels who 'evangelise' by proclaiming the Good News of Christ's Incarnation and Resurrection.[199] They will be present at Christ's return, which they will announce, to serve at his judgment.[200]

The Angels in the Life of the Church

334: In the meantime, the whole life of the Church benefits from the mysterious and powerful help of angels.[201]

335: In her Liturgy, the Church joins with the angels to adore the thrice-holy God. She invokes their assistance: in the Roman Canon's Supplices te rogamus... ("Almighty God, we pray that your angel..."); in the funeral liturgy's In Paradisum deducant te angeli...("May the angels lead you into Paradise..."). Moreover, in the 'Cherubic Hymn' of the Byzantine Liturgy, she celebrates the memory of certain angels more particularly (St. Michael, St. Gabriel, St. Raphael, and the guardian angels).

336: From infancy to death human life is surrounded by their watchful care and intercession.[202] Beside each believer stands an angel as protector and shepherd leading him to life.[203] Already here on earth the Christian life shares by faith in the blessed company of angels and men united in God.

The Fall of the Angels

391: Behind the disobedient choice of our first parents lurks a seductive voice, opposed to God, which makes them fall into death out of envy.[266] Scripture and the Church's Tradition see in this being a fallen angel, called 'Satan' or the 'devil'.[267] The Church teaches that Satan was at first a good angel, made by God: "The devil and the other demons were indeed created naturally good by God, but they became evil by their own doing".[268]

392: Scripture speaks of a sin of these angels.[269] This 'fall' consists in the free choice of these created spirits, who radically and irrevocably rejected God and his reign. We find a reflection of that rebellion in the tempter's words to our first parents: "You will be like God."[270] The devil "has sinned from the beginning"; he is "a liar and the father of lies".[271]

393: It is the irrevocable character of their choice, and not a defect in the infinite divine mercy, that makes the angels' sin unforgivable. There is no repentance for the angels after their fall, just as there is no repentance for men after death.[272]

394: Scripture witnesses to the disastrous influence of the one Jesus calls "a murderer from the beginning", who would even try to divert Jesus from the mission received from his Father.[273] The reason the Son of God appeared was to destroy the works of the devil.[274] In its consequences the gravest of these works was the mendacious seduction that led man to disobey God.

395: The power of Satan is, nonetheless, not infinite. He is only a creature, powerful from the fact that he is pure spirit, but still a creature. He cannot prevent the building up of God's reign. Although Satan may act in the world out of hatred for God and his kingdom in Christ Jesus, and although his action may cause grave injuries - of a spiritual nature, and indirectly, even of a physical nature - to each man and to society, the action is permitted by divine providence which with strength and gentleness guides human and cosmic history. It is a great mystery that providence should permit diabolical activity, but "we know that in everything God works for good for those who love him."[275] (Romans 8:28)

See references at the end of the chapter.

It would be possible to give a number of quotations from recent popes on angels and demons, but the following two passages will have to suffice: In his general audience on 15th November 1972 Pope Paul VI asked the question: "What are the greatest needs of the Church today?" This is how he replied: "Do not let our answer surprise you as being over simple or even superstitious and unreal: one of the greatest needs is defence from that evil which is called the Devil. Evil is not merely a lack of something, but an effective agent, a living, spiritual being, perverted and perverting. A terrible reality. It is contrary to the teaching of the Bible and the Church to refuse to recognise the existence of such a reality ... or to explain it as a pseudo reality, a conceptual and fanciful personification of the unknown causes of our misfortunes. That it is not a question of one devil, but of many, is indicated by the various passages in the Gospel (Luke 11:21; Mark 5:9). But the principal one is Satan, which means the adversary, the enemy; and with him many creatures of God, but fallen, because of their rebellion and damnation - a whole mysterious world, upset by the unhappy drama, of which we know very little." (L'Osservatore Romano 23rd November 1972).

In his general audience on 13th August 1986 Pope John Paul II said: "To conclude, we must add that the impressive words of the Apostle John,"The whole world lies under the power of the evil one" (1 John 5:19), allude also to the presence of Satan in the history of humanity, a presence which becomes all the more acute when man and society depart from God. The influence of the evil spirit can conceal itself in a more profound and effective way: it is in his 'interests' to make himself unknown. Satan has the skill to deny his existence in the name of rationalism and of every other system of thought which seeks all possible means to avoid recognising his activity. This, however, does not signify the elimination of man's free will and responsibility, and even less the frustration of the saving action of Christ. It is, rather, a case of a conflict between the dark powers of evil and the power of redemption."

Liturgy

In the liturgy of the Mass there are not a few references to angels. In one of the forms of the Penitential Rite we ask "all the angels and saints ... to pray for me to the Lord our God". In the Creed we say "we believe in God ... maker of all that is, seen and unseen" - the unseen being the angelic creation. In the Prefaces we join our prayer, with the angels, for example in Eucharistic

Prayer II: "And so we join the angels and the saints in proclaiming your glory as we sing: Holy, holy, holy...". In Eucharistic Prayer I, the priest says: "Almighty God, we pray that your angel may take this sacrifice to your altar in heaven".

On 29th September we celebrate the feast of the three Archangels, Michael, Gabriel, and Raphael. A few days later on October 2nd we have the Mass of the Guardian Angels. The Opening Prayer on 2nd October reads: "God our Father, in your loving providence you send your angels to watch over us. Hear our prayers, defend us always by their protection and let us share your life with them for ever". The hymn for the Morning Office of 2nd October is particularly beautiful:

"They come, God's messengers of love,
They come from realms of peace above,
From homes of never-fading light,
From blissful mansions ever bright.

They come to watch around us here,
To soothe our sorrow, calm our fear:
Ye heavenly guides, speed not away,
God willeth you with us to stay.

But chiefly at its journey's end
'Tis yours the spirit to befriend,
And whisper to the willing heart,
'O Christian soul, in peace depart.'

To us the seal of angels give,
With love to serve thee while we live;
To us an Angel-guard supply,
When on the bed of death we lie."

I cannot resist the temptation to quote also the inspiring Preface of the Angels:

"Father, all -powerful and ever-living God,
we do well always and everywhere to give you thanks.

In praising your faithful angels and archangels,
we also praise your glory,
for in honouring them, we honour you, their creator.
Their splendour shows us your greatness,
which surpasses in goodness the whole of creation.

Through Christ our Lord
the great army of angels rejoices in your glory.
In adoration and joy
we make their hymn of praise our own:

Holy, holy, holy ... "

I find myself wondering how a Catholic who dos not believe in the existence of personal angels feels as he or she hears the texts cited above in Mass. What sense does he or she make of it all? How can we ask God to "defend us always by their protection" if angels do not exist? How can we ask to "share your life with them for ever" in heaven if there are no personal angels? How can we praise "your faithful angels and archangels" in the Preface if they do not really exist?

At the Renewal of Baptismal promises in the Easter Vigil we are exhorted to "renew the promises we made in baptism when we rejected Satan and his works". These questions then follow: "Do you reject Satan? ... And all his works? ... And all his empty promises? ..." Or the celebrant can use alternative questions, which include: "Do you reject Satan, father of sin and prince of darkness?"

At baptisms there is the Prayer of Exorcism and Anointing before Baptism: "Almighty and ever-living God, you sent your only Son into the world to cast out the power of Satan, spirit of evil, to rescue man from the kingdom of darkness, and bring him into the splendour of your Kingdom of Light." And in the Rite of Christian Initiation of Adults, there are the prayers of Exorcism, one of which includes: "We pray for these your servants, who worship you as true God. Look upon them and enlighten their hearts, free them from the snares and malice of Satan, heal their weakness and blot out their sins".

Finally, at my funeral, God willing, they will sing or say the beautiful Antiphon: "May the angels lead you into paradise". May they be real angels!

References to the Quotations Given in Extracts from the Catechism of the Catholic Church

The Angels

188 St. Augustine En. in Ps 103, 1, 15: PL 37, 1348.
189 Mt 18:10; Ps 103:20.
190 Cf. Pius XII. Humani Generis. DS 3891. Lk 20:36; Dan 10: 9-12
191 Mt 25: 31.
192 Col 1:16.
193 Heb 1:14.
194 Cf. Job 38: 7 (where angels are called sons of God); Gen 3:24; 19; 21:17; 22:11; Acts 7:53; Ex 23:20-23; Judg 13;6:11-24; Is 6:6; 1 Kings 19:5.
195 Cf. Lk 1:11,26.
196 Heb 1:6.
197 Lk 2: 14.
198 Cf. Mt 1:20; 2:13,19; 4:11; 26:53; Mk 1:13; Lk 22: 43; 2 Macc 10:29-30; 11:8.
199 Cf. Lk 2:8-14; Mk 16:5-7.
200 Cf. Acts 1:10-11; Mt 13:41; 24:31; Lk 12:8-9.
201 Cf. Acts 5:18-20; 8:26-29;10:3-8;12:6-11; 27:23-25
202 Cf. Mt 18:10; Lk 16:22; Pss 34:7; 91:10-13; Job 33: 23-24; Zech 1:12; Tob 12:12.
203 St. Basil Adv. Eunomium III, 1: PG 29 656B.

The Fall of the Angels

266 Cf. Gen 3:1-5; Wis 2:24.
267 Cf. Jn 8:44; Rev 12:9.
268 Lateran Council IV (1215):DS 800.
269 Cf. 2 Pt 2:4.
270 Gen 3:5.
271 1 Jn 3:8; Jn 8:44.
272 St. John Damascene. De fide orth 2,4:PG 94, 877
273 Jn 8:44; Cf. Mt 4:1-11.
274 1 Jn 3:8.
275 Rom 8:28.

Appendix Two

The Saints and Demons

The lives and teachings of the saints are an important source of instruction on the subjects of angels, demons, and spiritual warfare. The saints are people who through the grace of God are special examples of how the Christian life should be lived - and when I use the word saint I am not only thinking of people who have been canonised, though in this Appendix I shall concentrate largely on them.

The saints over the centuries provide us with a great variety of ways of living the Christian life. Compare, for example, the life style of a Father of the Desert in the fifth century with that of a busy mother of a family in our own times. However, there are certain basic characteristics which are found in the life of every saint, whenever and wherever they lived. The saints were people of great faith, hope, love, and humility. The saints were truly men and women of prayer. And the saints recognised that they were involved in spiritual warfare.

As a monk I am very much aware that spiritual warfare against demonic forces is definitely a part of the monastic tradition. In the third century St. Anthony of Egypt, according to his life by St. Athanasius, was very much involved in fighting demons. It is recorded that he was even physically beaten by demons. And he was well known for his ministry of liberating people from demons. The monks, especially the hermits, were seen as going out into the desert to do battle with the devil with the aid of God's grace.

St. Benedict, who is called the Patriarch of Western Monasticism, lived in the fifth century and wrote a famous rule for monks and nuns. In the Prologue to this Rule, St. Benedict refers to the monk as "he that takes the evil spirit that tempts him, and casts him and his temptation from the sight of his heart, and brings him to nought; who grasps his evil suggestions as they arise and dashes them to pieces on the rock that is Christ". In the first chapter of the Rule, St. Benedict refers to hermits as "those who not in the first fervour of their conversion, but after long probation in a monastery, having learned in association with many brethren how to fight against the devil, go out well-armed from the ranks of the community to the solitary combat in the desert".

In St. Gregory the Great's short life of St. Benedict there are a considerable number of references to the devil. The devil is usually seen as tempting people and frequently as being cast out by St, Benedict. In chapter two we read that as a young man St. Benedict "was seized with an unusually violent temptation. The evil spirit recalled to his mind a woman he had once seen, and before he realised it, his emotions were carrying him away". St. Benedict overcame the temptation by rolling in nettles and briars, and never suffered from a temptation of that kind again. Note that it was the evil spirit who was seen as causing the temptation.

In chapter eight we learn that after St. Benedict

moved to Monte Cassino "the assaults he had to endure were all the more violent, because the very master of evil was fighting against him in open battle". St. Benedict had turned the temple of Apollo into a chapel dedicated to St. Martin. "Such losses the ancient enemy could not bear in silence. This time he did not appear to the saint in a dream or under a disguise but met him face to face and objected fiercely to the outrages he had to endure. His shouts were so loud that the brethren heard him too, although they were unable to see him". St. Benedict himself saw the devil, who had "an appearance utterly revolting to human eyes".

Some readers will doubtless wish to object that the extraordinary happenings recounted in ancient lives of the saints are to be regarded as legend not fact. I am not of course claiming that St. Athanasius' life of St. Anthony is to be considered entirely as history in the modern sense of the word. However, I do not think that all the extraordinary happenings there can simply be dismissed as legend. One reason for this is that extraordinary supernatural events are very much happening in our own times, where the evidence is convincing. So if Padre Pio was physically beaten by the devil, as we shall see later, then there is no reason to affirm that it did not happen to St. Anthony.

Some people who claim to be very reasonable, objective, and scientific are in fact prejudiced, unobjective, and unscientific when presented with evidence which goes contrary to their own preconceptions. Thus many people will, despite the evidence, dismiss all healing miracles because they do not believe that healing miracles could happen. One priest very much involved in psychology to whom I mentioned the case reported in the Introduction of a woman levitating when she was being exorcised simply replied: "I do not believe it happened." Because he did not believe that such a thing could happen, he simply dismissed the testimony of reliable people.

One could quote from the lives of so many saints on their experience of being attacked by demons whom they regarded as personal beings, not mythical ideas. For example, St. Francis of Assisi in the twelfth century was visiting Rome when, it is recorded: "The very first night he was there, when he had finished praying and was trying to get some rest, he was surrounded by devils who attacked him brutally. They beat him severely for a long time and then went off, leaving him half-dead".

St. Catherine of Siena in the 14th century, recounting a painful experience near the end of her life, wrote: "And then after a little the terror of the demons began so that I seemed to be stupefied. They were mad with rage, as though I, a worm, had been the cause of their having had the Holy Church which they were holding so long, snatched from their hands. And so great were both the terror and the physical pain that I wanted to fly from the study into the chapel".

St. Ignatius of Loyola, the founder of the Jesuits in the 16th century, meditates on the two standards, one of Christ, the other of Lucifer, in his famous Spiritual Exercises. Under the Standard of Satan he writes:

"FIRST PRELUDE. This is the history. Here it will be that Christ calls and wants all beneath His standard, and Lucifer, on the other hand, wants all under his.
SECOND PRELUDE. This is a mental representation of the place. It will be here to see a great plain, comprising the whole region about Jerusalem, where the sovereign Commander-in-Chief of all the good is Christ our Lord; and another plain about the region of Babylon, where the chief of the enemy is Lucifer.
THIRD PRELUDE. This is to ask for what I desire. Here it will be to ask for a knowledge of the deceits of the rebel chief and help to guard myself against them; and also to ask for a knowledge of the true life exemplified in the sovereign and true Commander, and the grace to imitate Him.

The Standard of Satan

FIRST POINT. Imagine you see the chief of all the enemy in the vast plain about Babylon, seated on a great throne of fire and smoke, his appearance inspiring horror and terror.
SECOND POINT. Consider how he summons innumerable demons, and scatters them, some to one city and some to another, throughout the whole world, so that no province, no place, no state of life, no individual is overlooked.
THIRD POINT. Consider the address he makes to them, how he goads them on to make snares for men and bind them with chains. First they are to tempt them to covet riches (as Satan himself is accustomed to do in most cases) that they may the more easily attain the empty honours of this world, and then come to

overweening pride.

The first step, then, will be riches, the second honour, the third pride. From these three steps the evil one leads to all other vices."

The two great Spanish Carmelite saints in the 16th century both wrote about the devil on many occasions. St. Teresa in her Life wrote: "It was only rarely that I saw Satan take a bodily form; I know of his presence through the vision I have spoken of before, the vision wherein no form is seen". St. John of the Cross wrote of the devil in the Spiritual Canticle: "There is no human power that can be compared with his, and thus only the divine power suffices to be able to conquer him, and the divine light alone to penetrate his wiles".

The above quotations are short snippets in passing, which amongst other things, show clearly that the saints in question really believed in the existence of personal demons. Now I want us to look at greater length at the demonic experiences of St. John Vianney, the Curé d'Ars (1786-1859), a very great saint who lived nearer to our times and concerning whose life there is plenty of historical evidence. I am quoting at some length from the well-known biography, 'The Curé d'Ars', by Abbé Francis Trochu, (TAN Books). This book devotes a whole chapter to 'The Curé d'Ars and the Devil.'

"For the space of some 35 years - from 1824-1858 - the Curé d'Ars was subjected, even outwardly, to the molestations of the evil one. What if, by preventing him from taking both food and sleep, Satan had succeeded in inspiring him with a distaste for prayer, penance, and the exertions of the apostolic life, and in obliging him to give up the cure of souls! But the enemy of our salvation was disappointed and defeated. 'The struggles of M.Vianney with the devil,' said Catherine Lassagne, 'helped to render his charity more evident and more disinterested.'

"It was indeed a battle, and in order to fight it the holy man had no other resource than patience and prayer. 'I sometimes asked him', his confessor relates, 'how he repelled these attacks.' He replied: 'I turn to God; I make the sign of the cross; I address a few contemptuous words to the devil. I have noticed, moreover, that the tumult is greater and the assaults more numerous if, on the following day, some big sinner is due to come'. "

This knowledge was his comfort during sleepless nights. "At the beginning I felt afraid," he confessed to Mgr. Mermod, one of his friends and faithful penitents; "I did not then know what it was, but now I am quite happy. It is a good sign: there is always a good haul of fish the next day." "The devil gave me a good shaking last night," he would say at times; "we shall have a great number of people tomorrow. The grappin is very stupid: he himself tells me of the arrival of big sinners .... He is angry. So much the better!"

It is also recorded that "the evil spirit remained invisible, but his presence could be plainly felt. He threw over the chairs and shook the heavy furniture of the room. With a fearful voice he shouted: 'Vianney,

Vianney! potato eater! Ah! thou art not yet dead! I shall get thee all right'. Or, roaring like a beast, growling like a bear, or snarling like a dog, he rushed at the curtains of the bed, which he shook violently."

Borrowing from the accounts of Catherine Lassagne and from his own recollections, Frère Athanase relates that the devil "reproduced the sound of a hammer driving nails into the wooden floor, or that of hooping a cask; he drummed on the table, on the chimney-piece, on the water jug; or he sang with a shrill voice, so that M.le Curé used afterwards to tell us derisively: 'The grappin has a very ugly voice indeed.'

"On more than one occasion M.Vianney experienced a sensation as of a hand passing over his face or of rats scampering over his body.

"One night he heard the buzz of a swarm of bees; he got up, lit his candle, and was about to open the window to let them out - but he saw no bees.

"Another time the grappin endeavoured to throw him out of bed by pulling away his straw mattress. More frightened than usual, M. Vianney crossed himself, and the devil left him in peace."

It is important to remember that other people also heard the sounds and saw the physical chaos caused by the devil. The Curé's sister, for example, when visiting him was frightened when she heard a "tremendous noise". The Curé said to her: "O my child! you should not have been frightened: it is the grappin. He cannot hurt you: as for me, he torments me in sundry ways. At times he seizes me by the feet and drags me about the room. It is because I convert souls to the good God."

Then there was the occasion when a mysterious fire broke out in the Curé's room. His bed was burned, but inexplicably the fire did not spread to other things. The fire started without any apparent human cause, and ended inexplicably. It was regarded by the Curé and others as an attack of the devil.

Two other points must be mentioned in passing. The Curé was, with the permission of the local bishop, very active in the ministry of exorcism. There are numerous accounts of people delivered by him from evil spirits. The other point is that the Curé was severe about involvement in spiritualism and the occult. Problems to do with involvement in spiritualism and the occult are not new!

Let us now consider the cases of two Catholics who lived in this century who were both the object of violent attacks by the devil - and both of whose canonisation causes have been officially introduced. The first is the famous Italian Capuchin, Padre Pio (1887-1968), whose funeral was attended by 100,000 people. In his book, 'Padre Pio. The True Story', Bernard Ruffin writes : "Because of his intense spiritual life, Padre Pio saw manifestations of supernatural power where many would not. For instance, in August 1912, for a space of several days, whenever he began to write to his superiors, he was seized with violent migraine headaches and spasms in his writing arm. Recognising this as devilish interference, he prayed and was able to write again. Many of the unseen attacks were in the form of temptations against purity.

"Many of the diabolical attacks, however, were

quite physical and were accompanied by terrifying noises that could be heard by neighbours. Pio was struck by actual blows that left visible bruises. Padre Pio continued to receive visits from his guardian angel, as well as from Jesus and Mary."

Bernard Ruffin gives more than one example of these attacks. "The community sat down to eat, while Pio, as usual, remained upstairs in bed. During the course of the meal, everyone heard a terrific crash, just as if, as Paolino put it, a huge drum of gasoline had been dropped from a height and had crashed to the floor. Immediately Paolino ran upstairs to find Pio pale and drenched in perspiration, as if he had gone swimming in his nightshirt. The same thing happened for several successive nights."

Here is a final incident: "That night Padre Pio was alone in his room. At ten o'clock some of his colleagues heard a terrific crash. Running to his room, they found the padre on the floor in a pool of blood. His face was swollen and discoloured, and he was bleeding profusely from his nose and from a deep cut on his forehead. There were no signs of forced entry, nothing was broken, and everything was in its usual place except for a pillow that, instead of being in Pio's armchair was neatly tucked beneath the old man's bleeding head.

"The guardian, Padre Carmelo of San Giovanni in Galdo, asked who had put the pillow under his head. Weakly, Pio replied, 'The Madonna.'

"Padre Pio's injuries were real. His gash required stitches. For five days he could not celebrate Mass in public. As Father Joseph Pius recalls: "His face was cut above the right eyebrow. His eyes were black, all black under the eyes. His shoulders were terribly bruised. I saw it."

It should also be mentioned that a considerable number of people were delivered from evil spirits through the ministry of Padre Pio.

The second person is Marthe Robin (1902-1981), a French woman who, like Padre Pio, received the stigmata, and who played a key role in the foundation of lay communities. For fifty years she lay paralysed on her bed, for about the last forty of which she was blind, and she neither ate - apart from Holy Communion - drank, or slept for many years. Five bishops and two hundred priests were present at her funeral.

Marthe Robin was very much involved in spiritual warfare with the devil, and this also, amongst other things, took the form of physical attacks. Frequently the furniture in her room was thrown about and this paralysed woman was sometimes half thrown out of her bed. Indeed, when she was found dead her body was lying on the floor. No human being had entered the room, and as a very paralysed person she could not possibly have moved from the bed.

Some readers may think that in this chapter I have concentrated too much on the physical attacks of the devil. After all, are not the spiritual aspects of demonic attacks more important and far more common? Yes. But people who do not believe in the existence of personal demons will psychologically explain away the spiritual attacks as something purely natural and human. It is however difficult to explain away the physical attacks of the devil such as those mentioned in this chapter. The historical evidence is surely very clear for the Curé d'Ars, Padre Pio, and Marthe Robin. Some theologians regard the devil and demons as myths. But myths do not create loud noises, set beds on fire, throw people around, or inflict wounds that have to be stitched.

Some people may wish to suggest that these three were psychologically sick people suffering from hallucinations and that their followers were caught up in some form of collective hysteria. Hallucinations and hysteria, however, do not result in the extraordinary apostolic fruitfulness, including many lasting conversions and physical miracles, such as we see in the lives of the Curé d'Ars, Padre Pio, and Marthe Robin. "Thus you will know them by their fruits". (Matthew 7:20).

Appendix Three

The Saints and Angels

In the last chapter we have been dealing with the fallen angels, not the glorious ones. Experience of demons is much more common than experience of good angels in the lives of the saints and other Christians. The reason for this is surely that on the positive side, the experience of Jesus himself and of his mother are much more frequent and are what dominates. Many Christians have had some kind of experience of Jesus who have never been aware of the presence of angels. Nevertheless there have been a very considerable number of reports of the experience of angels in the lives of the saints and other Christians.

In the Acts of the Apostles (Chapter 27, verse 22) Paul said to the men in danger of shipwreck: "I urge you now to keep up your courage, for there will be no loss of life among you, but only of the ship. For last night there stood by me an angel of the God to whom I belong and whom I worship, and he said, 'Do not be afraid, Paul, you must stand before the emperor; and indeed, God has granted safety to all who are sailing with you' ". As we shall see, angelic appearances and messages like this one to St. Paul did not end with the New Testament. The following pages give a small sample of these.

St. Benedict (480-c.550) in a vision "saw the soul of

Germanus, the Bishop of Capua, being carried by angels up to heaven in a ball of fire" - subsequent enquiry revealed that the bishop had died at the time of the vision.

A number of the early martyrs of the Church were reported to have been helped by angels in their martyrdoms. St. Theodosius said that "an Angel came to my side and refreshed my burning wounds". Three angels appeared to St. Eulalia and comforted her with consoling words. St. Vincent was also comforted by angels, with whom he sang the praises of God. One of the soldiers present at the martyrdom of St. Lawrence saw an angel, and this led to his conversion.

Angels appeared more than once to St. Dominic (1170-1221) and to some of his brethren. When St. Francis of Assisi (1181-1226) received the stigmata on Mount Alverna, a seraph "with six resplendent and flaming wings" came to him.

Michael the Archangel is said to have appeared several times at a cave on Monte Gargano in Italy, starting in the fifth century. There is now a sanctuary there dedicated to him. Another shrine was built in the eighth century at Mount-Saint-Michel in France following an apparition of St. Michael to a bishop. St. Joan of Arc (1412-1431) saw the Archangel Michael frequently, and at her trial, at which she was wrongly condemned, the judges tried to persuade her that she had been seeing the devil disguised as St. Michael.

St. Frances of Rome (1384-1440) for many years was accustomed to seeing her guardian angel at her side. She described him in these words: "His aspect is full of sweetness and majesty; his eyes are generally turned toward Heaven; words cannot describe the divine purity of that gaze. His brow is always serene; his glances kindle in the soul the flame of ardent devotion. When I look upon him, I understand the glory of the angelic nature, and the degraded condition of our own. He wears a long shining robe and over it a tunic, either as white as the lilies of the field or of the colour of a red rose or of the hue of the sky when it is most deeply blue. When he walks by my side, his feet are never soiled by the mud of the streets or the dust of the road".

Two other saints nearer our own times had remarkable experiences. St. John Bosco (1815-1888) was on a number of occasions protected by a large black dog when he was making dangerous journeys. The dog, which he called Grigio, mysteriously appeared when needed and equally mysteriously vanished when the danger was over. Was the dog a protecting angel? St. Gemma Galgani (1878-1903) was, like St. Frances of Rome, constantly able to see her guardian angel, with whom she chatted familiarly. She once said when referring to her sufferings caused by illness: "How could I have ever borne those awful pains had it not been for the presence of my Angel?"

In 1916 the Angel Guardian of Portugal appeared three times to the three child visionaries in Fatima. Sister Lucy writes: "Suddenly, though the day was very mild, a strong wind began to sway the branches of the tree and we glanced up to see the cause of it. We saw over the trees a light as white as snow and in the midst of it the form of a young man as brilliant as crystal, as when it is lit up by the light of the sun. As he approached us, we began to see his features clearly. We were surprised, absorbed by what we saw, but we said not a word. On coming near us he said, 'Do not be afraid, I am the Angel of Peace. Pray with me.' " In the three appearances the angel taught them to pray and spiritually guided them. Of course some people will say that all this was just the imagination of young children or made up by them to attract attention. But these three visits of the angel resulted in very remarkable spiritual growth - and such growth would not have followed purely human imagination or invention.

Padre Pio (1887-1968) had a strong devotion to the angels, especially his guardian angel. Indeed, a whole book has been written on his relationship with the angels, whom he saw frequently in visions: "Send Me Your Guardian Angel", by Fr. Alessio Parente OFM.Cap. Padre Pio used to tell his spiritual children to "send me your guardian angel" when they were in trouble. He once said to someone: "Didn't you see all those Guardian Angels going backwards and forwards from my spiritual children bringing messages from them?" Padre Pio wrote in a letter: "On the 20th of this month I offered the Holy Sacrifice for you. My good Guardian Angel knows this and I have entrusted him many times with the delicate task of coming to console you". Fr. Alessio Parente writes: "Obviously for Padre Pio, after Jesus and Mary came his Guardian Angel, who played a very important role in his sanctification and mission. He and his Guardian Angel are so closely linked with one another that it is impossible to separate them. His Angel knew how to guide, enlighten, and direct him along the difficult path to sanctity, and Padre Pio was a very docile instrument in his hands".

The wife of an Anglican vicar, Hope Price, has produced a remarkable book of accounts of contemporary Christians' experiences of angels: 'Angels - True Stories of How they Touch our Lives' (MacMillan 1993). After feeling moved by the Lord to undertake this venture, she placed notices in Christian papers asking people who had experiences of angels to send her accounts. Large numbers of Christians replied to this request, and after careful discernment she put many accounts together in the form of a book. From reading this book one realises that apparitions of angels to Christians are obviously happening in our times, and not so infrequently. There is a striking similarity between some of these accounts - one might say that there seem to be four main categories of experience.

In the first, the angels are seen in traditional form with wings, and often glowing with light. In the second category, the angels appear as ordinary human beings, perform an act of service, and then usually suddenly and inexplicably vanish when their task is completed. In the third group, the angels are not seen or heard, but their presence is deduced from what happened, for example, a car is inexplicably saved from a bad accident as if by unseen hands. Finally, in a fourth set of experiences, people hear heavenly singing - a friend of mine told me that when her grandmother was dying she and her mother who were praying in the room heard the most wonderful heavenly singing and music for about ten to fifteen minutes. I will add that quite a number of the accounts in the book concern dying people - the angels appear as if to lead them to heaven.

There is one case in this book on which I would like to expand, that of an Anglican woman, Dorothy Kerin (1890-1963). On February 17th 1912 she was dying, after having been bed-ridden for five years - the doctor did not think she would survive the night. She had received Holy Communion on 4th February and she and her sister then heard what they were convinced was angelic singing; then she became unconscious. She had a vision of a "wonderful altar, formed as it were by angels.........As I looked I saw one coming towards me. I thought he was coming for me and held out my hands towards him, but he smiled and said, 'No, Dorothy, you are not coming yet'." Then she heard a voice saying "Dorothy" three times. "I answered, 'Yes, I am listening. Who is it?' Then a great light came around me and an angel took my hand in his and said, 'Dorothy, your sufferings are over. Get up and walk'. He passed his hands over my eyes and touched my ears, and then I opened my eyes and found myself sitting up in bed ... The angel again said to me: 'Get up and walk'. They brought the dressing-gown. When I had put it on I got out of bed unassisted. Part of the light which emanated from the angel came to the right side of my bed. I put my hand on it, and it led me out of the room, along a passage and back into my bedroom. Though I had not walked for nearly five years, I now walked quite steadily, not the least bit shaky; indeed I felt well and strong and might never have been ill at all." Her emaciated, discoloured, and skeleton-like body was immediately restored to a normal, plump, healthy condition. The tubercular meningitis and other illnesses had disappeared immediately.

I have chosen to mention these apparitions of angels to Dorothy Kerin at some length for two reasons. First, her immediate healing was surely one of the most remarkable healing miracles ever recorded - and the medical evidence for the healing is overwhelming. Secondly, because after later receiving the stigmata Dorothy became one of the main pioneers of the renewal of the healing ministry in the Christian Church. She went on to found the well-known healing centre at Burrswood (Kent), which is still flourishing today. So her miraculous healing by Jesus, which was linked with the apparitions of angels, led to a life and ministry of very exceptional fruitfulness for the Kingdom of God. False apparitions or hysterical imagination would not have led to such great fruitfulness.

It makes me sad to think of Christians who do not believe in angels. Of course, Jesus, not angels, is the centre of our faith. But what a pity not to be aware of the protecting angels whom Jesus has given us and not to look forward to praising God with the angels in heaven, later!

Further copies of **"I Saw Satan Fall"**
and other books by Dom Benedict Heron:
Praying for Healing, the challenge
Come Holy Spirit, help us to pray
are available from the retail division of
New Life Publishing:

Goodnews Books & Audio
60 Wickstead Avenue,
Luton, Beds. LU4 9DP
Tel: 01582 571011 Fax: 01582 571012
email: orders@goodnewsbooks.net
www.goodnewsbooks.net

other New Life titles also available:
God is a Feast - an introduction to St. John of the Cross
by Fr. Pius Sammut OCD, translated by mark Agius MD
Joy in Heaven by Luke Bell OSB

NOTES

NOTES

NOTES

NOTES

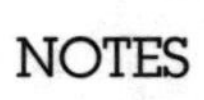

NOTES

NOTES

NOTES